This is the story of a land and its people, a story of diversity and change in the midst of loyalty and tradition, a fond portrait in pictures and words of the many faces of South Carolina, by the authors of *The Goodliest Land: North Carolina.*

Known for its magnificent ante-bellum plantation houses, its beautiful landscaped gardens (*"Gardening and the appreciation of beauty are a way of life"*), the rolling countryside of the upcountry, and the tree-lined streets of its small towns, South Carolina is also fast becoming an industrial center — of the fifty states only three have more international companies than South Carolina.

Mirroring the variety of its landscape is the diversity of its people. And this is primarily a book about people, from those who founded "Charles Town" over three-hundred years ago and transformed it into the "London of the New World," to those who fought bravely in the Revolutionary War (including Francis Marion, the "Swamp Fox"), those (such as General Wade Hampton) whose courage and resilience helped to pull South Carolina out of the desolation of Reconstruction, to the people of South Carolina today, whose vitality, dedication to preserving the beauties of the past, and plans for the future make

South Carolina one of the mo_____ ing places in the United States to ▲

The spirit of the land and the people is captured here in vivid descriptions, interviews with proud citizens, and Bruce Roberts' thoughtful photographs.

Nancy Roberts is best known for her books on Carolina ghosts, but has also written half a dozen other books including *Where Time Stood Still: A Portrait of Appalachia* and *Sense of Discovery: The Mountain.*

Bruce Roberts' photographs have appeared in many national publications, and he has twice been named Southern Photographer of the Year. Among his previous books is *The Carolina Gold Rush, America's First.* The husband and wife team have also coauthored two children's books, *America's Most Haunted Places* and *Ghosts of the Wild West.* They live in Charlotte, North Carolina.

THE FACES
OF
SOUTH CAROLINA

THE FACES
OF
SOUTH
CAROLINA

Text by NANCY ROBERTS

Photographs by BRUCE ROBERTS

24372

Doubleday & Company, Inc., Garden City, New York   1976

Library of Congress Cataloging in Publication Data

Roberts, Bruce, 1930–
    The faces of South Carolina.

    1. South Carolina—Description and travel—
1951– 2. South Carolina—History. I. Roberts,
Nancy, 1924–   joint author. II. Title.
F275.R62   975.7
ISBN 0-385-07752-1
Library of Congress Catalog Card Number 75–40741

Dedicated to William Smith and his ancestors
and those like them who followed Francis Marion,
Sumter, and Pickens through the swamps
and palmetto thickets and to the tops of the Carolina mountains
until they had chased the last English flag
from the state and replaced it with the banner of liberty.

CONTENTS

———◆———

THE FACES
OF
SOUTH CAROLINA

AS LONG AS THIS LAND
SHALL LAST

◆

South Carolina is another world, a different country from the rest of the nation in many ways. Its land is as diverse as its people, ranging from semitropical islands off the coast to the mountains of the Blue Ridge.

The state is pie-shaped with rolling hills at the edge of the broad portion of the triangle merging into mountains to the west along the North Carolina border. South of these hills and mountains are the rolling red clay fields of the upcountry. Midway in the state the red clay disappears and there are sand hills before the land slopes toward the sea to become fertile coastal plains.

Over three hundred years ago, one hundred forty-eight English colonists established the first settlement near the coast on the Ashley River. They named it Charles Town in honor of their king and it was destined to become the London of the New World. Many of these settlers were educated, wealthy aristocrats who followed the form of government and social customs of England. In this humid, semitropical land of palm trees, live oaks, Spanish moss, and bougainvillaea, they developed a merchant-planter society, dividing the land in the manner of English baronial estates.

Drained by three main rivers, the Pee Dee in the northeast, the Santee in the central area, and the Savannah in the southwest, the swift flow was to mean power for industry in the upcountry and river highways for the low country. As the rivers approach the coast they widen and are ideal for navigation. Beside their amber-colored waters, tinted by tannic acid from the roots of cyprus trees, magnificent, white-columned plantation homes began to rise from misty, green marshlands. Along the rivers went indigo, rice, and bales of cotton to the port of Charleston.

As the early planters acquired thousands of acres of land, the need for labor became more acute. The arrival of the first New England slave ships brought strong backs to till the fields and on every plantation small brick or white frame cabins sprang up. The Africans were trained in cultivating crops, carpentry, weaving, smithery and all the skills that a community of several hundred or a thousand or more people depended upon. Each plantation became a community filling its own needs with a minimum of dependence upon the outside world.

Charleston was both the home and meeting place for some of the

An avenue of oaks leads up to a plantation house near Georgetown.

The outlines of the original brick slave cabins are seen on a rainy day at Boone Hall Plantation at Mount Pleasant.

greatest minds of the colonies. To this center of society and culture came statesmen, writers, artists, and thinkers. Here was established the first public library, the first free school for blacks, the first musical society, the first opera performance, and the first theater which to this day still flourishes—the Old Dock Street Theater.

An interesting story is told of President Washington's trip to Charleston where he was lavishly entertained. A state banquet was one of the events planned. The committee was eager that President Washington have a good time and they were undecided about the seating arrangements. The governor's lady would, of course, be on his right but who would be his other companions? A clever sailor named Commodore Gillon came to the rescue. He chose Mrs. Richard Shubrick, the most beautiful woman in Charleston, to sit across from him and on his left he seated Miss Claudia Smith, the wittiest.

The plantations prospered and, until the time of the Revolution, the number of slaves continued to rise in South Carolina, although fears of possible revolts were ever present. When it was noticed that the insurrections were usually led by blacks of some learning, the efforts to educate them for the most part ceased.

At Stono, South Carolina, in 1739, "A great number of Negroes rose in rebellion, broke open a store where they got arms, killed twenty-one white persons and were marching the next morning out of the province, killing all they met and burning several houses as they passed along the road," before they were apprehended. The 22,000 Negroes in the province far outnumbered the whites, probably by three to one. Four years after the Stono insurrection, a law was passed requiring men to go armed to church in readiness for an uprising.

Despite this fear, slaves were trained to bear arms. Some served against the Spaniards in 1742, and many served in the Revolution and were freed because of their war record. Before 1800 there were hundreds of free blacks in South Carolina. A few of them owned plantations and slaves, but most were artisans supporting themselves with the skills they had been taught before they became free men.

A group of freed men of mixed blood organized a society later called the Century Fellowship Society to educate and help other Negroes. Unfortunately, prejudice based on skin color kept the lighter group from associating with darker-skinned Negroes or permitting them to use their banks, churches, and schools. Although the Century Fellowship Society is no more, some of this prejudice still results in social discrimination in the Charleston of today.

The native Charlestonian, both black and white, is proud of the beauty of his city, imbued with a sense of its history, and fundamentally conservative in both dress and political views. There is considerable caution when

It really is a scene from Gone with the Wind. *When they made the movie, some of the outside photography was at Boone Hall, and Tara was modeled after Boone Hall.*

A small protest by a taxpayer is written on the inside of the bridge.

Prather's Bridge which connects South Carolina with Georgia has almost as many lives as a cat. First built in 1804, it was burned during the war in 1863, rebuilt, then washed out by a flood in 1918, and currently is using its third life.

Long Cane Covered Bridge near Mount Carmel, another of the few remaining covered bridges in the state.

something new is proposed and the ideas and values of the past are not readily discarded.

Old families still exert considerable influence but it is now tempered with that of the military establishment and academic community from The Citadel, the College of Charleston, which is the oldest municipal college in the United States, and the Medical University. The Citadel exemplifies what is best in the military tradition of the South and South Carolina. Founded in 1842, it has been the source of distinguished officers for the Confederacy, for the war with Spain, and for World Wars I and II. "It was a cadet battery that fired the first gun of the War for Southern Independence" and the cadets who drove off the Union ship *Star of the West* which was attempting to bring supplies to the besieged garrison at Fort Sumter. Since its reopening in 1882 (it had been occupied by Union soldiers) the Citadel has bred a remarkable number of government leaders.

Charleston is queen of the low country, her sparkling diadem the bridges of the Ashley and Cooper rivers by night. She has survived hurricanes, floods, and fires. Federal-period mansions are still elegant, and many of them have domestic buildings (once used for slaves) attached to the great houses. The buildings of the business district are full of interesting

If John Henry's ghost ever needs a new home, Stumphouse Tunnel in Oconee County would be the place. Here they didn't use steam drills and the hand-drill marks may still be seen in the granite tunnel. In the 1850s four sections of tunnel were started but none was ever connected and the Blue Ridge Railroad was a casualty of the war between the states. The Stumphouse Tunnel is the only portion that is open and 1,600 feet are lighted. There are picnic tables and a small campground at the entrance.

architectural detail. The atmosphere of the 1800s that surrounds the visitor to Charleston is undoubtedly its greatest attraction—even Williamsburg cannot match these homes and buildings so full of history and the vitality which daily usage and living in them brings.

Along the rivers of the low country are scores of fine ante-bellum plantation homes. Some are still in the families of native South Carolinians, but many have been sold to wealthy Northerners. Georgetown and Beaufort as well as Charleston are famous for their magnificent old homes.

The men of the upcountry were a different breed from those who settled in Charleston. They came from Scotland and Ireland, overland through Pennsylvania, Virginia, and North Carolina. They lived hard and dan-

Fort Hill, the home of John C. Calhoun, is surrounded by Clemson College. At the peak of his career Calhoun resigned as Vice President of the United States and entered the Senate as the elected spokesman of South Carolina. It was his belief that no state was bound by a federal law which it believed unconstitutional. He felt that South Carolina was exploited by powerful New England lobbies in Congress that protected manufacturing interests in New England while economically damaging the southern economy.

Richard Petty, the winningest stock car driver in history, zips by a Confederate flag in his famous Plymouth with the number 43 on the side.

The Darlington Raceway is the granddaddy of stock car racing. In the late fifties, when the picture above was taken at the Rebel 500 race, the infield was filled mostly with cars and a few trucks. By 1975 the infield appears to be a rally of recreational vehicles.

gerously, fighting the Indians and carving small farms out of the land. Many worked with their own hands believing slavery morally wrong.

For a long time these men from the upcountry had little influence or voice in South Carolina's Commons House. Nor did this improve until they won the bitter contest over removal of the state capital from Charleston to Columbia in 1786. This was a convenient location for all South Carolinians.

Two discoveries bound the upcountry and the low country closer together—the invention of the cotton gin and the discovery that cotton would grow in the red clay north of the sandhills. With the coming of the white fields to the hills and valleys of the Piedmont came slaves. The obsession with cotton and the creation of a cotton empire had begun. By 1860 southern cotton accounted for 57 per cent of all American exports. The South was important to the nation and to European countries as well.

But tragedy was already imminent. Radical and fanatic men in the North and hotheads in the South were moving toward confrontation. Moderate men pleaded but their voices were swept away by the sound and the fury of the gathering storm. Those men in South Carolina who loved the Union and wished to settle differences with reason rather than saber and gunpowder were either ignored or challenged to a duel. Wade Hampton, who had recently addressed the legislature urging peace and reason, did not attend the special session called by Governor Pickens for the purpose of discussing secession. Hampton neither approved of secession nor admired Pickens. On December 20, 1860, the legislature of South Carolina voted to secede from the Union.

In the early months of the war, victory seemed to follow victory for the South but greatly superior numbers and the material resources available to the Union troops gradually began to tell. As the war drew to a close, South Carolina was doomed to worse pillage and ruin than any other southern state. Whole districts were burned bare with hardly a trace of anything living left. Roads were often impassable. Stores were closed for lack of stock to sell. Blacks and whites alike suffered. Without food, many of the physically weak died. Columbia's famous poet, Henry Timrod, before his death in 1867, wrote to a friend describing the past year. "I can embody it all in a few words, beggary, starvation, death, bitter grief, utter want of hope!"

Basically, the war had been an effort by the North to gain by force what they had been unable to do by politics. To give a free hand to the thievish aims of the northeastern tariff gang and to exercise that instinctive urge of men to put down whatever differs from themselves. And there existed on the part of many, a particular hatred of anything aristocratic, anything which in character, education, or way of life might seem superior to them.

The discovery that the southern mind, far from being smashed, was reinforced and confirmed through this war was a bitter revelation, and the Yankee came back to harry the South with bayonets, threats, and looting.

At places like Kingstree and Middleton gardens there are jousting tournaments. The knights on horseback are decked out in colorful finery instead of armor and charge down a path spearing rings on their lances. It is a skill demanding the utmost co-ordination of horse and rider, but it is also a social event. The ladies are elaborately gowned and dances and parties accompany the sporting event. A knight and his horse and a driver and his stock car—each share a special sort of excitement and competition.

To South Carolina came natives of New England and the Midwest to govern the state by means of intimidation and political machinations. Eleven years of military occupation, chaos, and corruption followed.

The first step on the long road back began with the election of General Wade Hampton as governor in 1876. If South Carolina had been in a state of ruin at the close of the war, Hampton found it, if anything, worse off. There were overdue salaries to teachers to be paid, institutions like the insane asylum without funds to continue operating, and a huge public debt, the heritage of graft and profligacy.

Hampton held firmly to his policy of nondiscrimination toward blacks as he had promised before his election. His reorganized militia included a regiment of black infantry at Charleston; at the same time the Connecticut legislature was refusing to approve a Negro militia company!

In speaking to his war comrades, Hampton said, "As a slave he was faithful to us. As a freedman, let us treat him as a friend." Others felt kindly toward the blacks, but at that time no one else seems to have been as outspoken an advocate of Negro citizenship rights. The greatest bitterness, however, was not toward the blacks but the Yankees.

When did the first Southerner shake the first Yankee hand after he had sworn he would never do such a thing if he lived to be a hundred? Perhaps it was the hand of General O. O. Howard in 1876. General Wade Hampton was visiting in Columbia and met him at the home of a friend, Major Gibbes. The major introduced them and Howard offered his one remaining hand. In one of his rare moments of anger, Hampton replied coldly, "I cannot take your hand, sir, until you retract your statement as to my connection with the burning of this city." Hampton had withdrawn from his home city of Columbia shortly before Sherman entered it. The Union hero responded promptly: "I fully admit that I was mistaken in that matter, and I hope you will forgive and forget." He offered his hand once more. This time Hampton grasped it and the two men became friends.

As the 1880s arrived a great dream formed in the minds of the leaders of South Carolina and was shared by other southern states. It spread among the people as a fire spreads through a pine forest and soon everyone was convinced that the road to wealth, education, and progress for the South was to build textile mills. The Charleston *News and Courier* editorialized about it, orators exhorted, and ministers preached from the pulpit that the most Christian thing one could do was to start a textile mill!

Even the poor, who could not possibly have bought a share of stock, formed pools paying in twenty-five cents a week. Enthusiasm spread from one community to another and, although the land was stripped of capital, from 1880 to 1900 a hundred textile mills were built in South Carolina. The Southerner has a genius for action. He is no alienated man; the belief that

God wants him to do something and that it will benefit his town are all he needs to know.

With the arrival of the mills, hundreds of men, women, and children left their hoes and plows for the heat and noise of the textile mills. Here was a new opportunity but wages remained low and the mill villages trapped many for generations. Said one old man, "When my children went into the mills we didn't know the village schools would make 'em different—them and their children." But it did, and for these children, just as for those in the heavily industrialized North, there was little education until child labor laws were passed.

Now, there are many modern mills with profit-sharing plans and better job opportunities for their employees. An economy once predominantly textile is passing, along with the demise of the mill village. The single largest employer is still the textile industry, but there are also metalwork, paper, chemical and allied companies, and South Carolina is becoming a favorite location for international investors. Of the fifty states, only three have more international companies than South Carolina.

In addition to alluring tax advantages, the state recruits and trains workers at no cost to the company. Five major interstate highways, two major railroads, ninety-two airports, and three major seaports, Charleston, Georgetown, and Port Royal are some of the attractions.

But the most valuable resource is the people. South Carolinians believe in the dignity of work and take pride in doing a good job. Their positive attitude toward industry is reflected by increased productivity and product quality. Industrial growth in South Carolina has been of a sufficient amount and variety for the state to now concentrate on encouraging industries with high wage scales and minimum impact on the environment.

Just forty-five minutes south of the megalopolis of Charlotte, North Carolina, are verdant fields of soybeans, beautiful, rolling pastureland dotted with black Angus cattle, hillsides a solid drift of pink peach blossoms and flourishing vineyards. This is the rural South Carolina upcountry north of the capital city of Columbia.

It is the setting for numerous small towns with tree-lined streets and so little traffic that it is safe to stare at the handsome pre-Civil War mansions while driving through. There are towns named York, Lancaster, and Chester. If these names sound familiar, it is because they were settled by Pennsylvanians who named them after the towns they left behind them.

Moving South before the Revolution, the newcomers readily adapted to an agrarian way of life. Some acquired slaves along with large landholdings and built plantation houses almost as elaborate as those in the low country. Many were Patriots in the Revolution, distinguishing themselves for their courage. And almost a century later they fiercely resisted the Yankees in the "War of Northern Aggression."

Boone Hall Plantation near Mount Pleasant is the classic southern plantation.

The atmosphere is peaceful, the pace leisurely, the buildings from the Revolutionary and ante-bellum periods still in use and it sometimes seems the "Confederate War" was yesterday and the Revolution the day before! They cannot have been too long ago, for the man who waits upon you in the hardware store or the local newspaper editor recall just what Cornwallis and Sherman did and said when they came through here. They mention it as they might recount the events of last night's PTA meeting to a friend. If you think that several later wars have erased the tracks of history from their soil or minds, you are not yet in tune with the time mechanism of the warm and friendly people around you. It is not so much that animosities live on in South Carolina, but rather that memories refuse to die.

A former weekly newspaper editor, G. M. Ketchin, talking about his native Winnsboro, pauses, "Before you leave, just one thing more. One of our men here was in the battle of the Wilderness and a bullet hit his forehead traveling the length of his scalp. Despite his wound he raised his hand in the air beckoning to his men and called out, 'Charge, boys. Remember where you're from!'"

Remember . . . remember. It is characteristic of the South Carolinian that he remembers where he is from. There are close ties and a loyalty to family, peer group, the land, and his state. At the same time he feels free to be outspokenly critical, particularly of events at the state level.

Few South Carolinians really enjoy city life. "I used to work in Charlotte, but I didn't know the neighbors on either side. That isn't for me," says the manager of a furniture store in York. "I want to live where people know each other and care what happens to them." Those who live in the cities for business reasons see the influence of the small town as good: "Our churches still play an important part in our lives, bringing the thoughtfulness and sense of community from the small towns into the life of our cities."

Many rural South Carolina communities enjoy well-stocked small libraries, discussion groups, and little theater societies providing more cultural opportunity than one might expect. These towns are home for the South Carolinians who commute to work in the larger cities such as Charleston in the low country and Greenville and Columbia in the Piedmont.

A drive through the upcountry is fully as rewarding as a tour of low country. Rural roads wind through rolling, pleasant farm country dotted with lakes and ponds. "These are fair fields," said Cornwallis as he traveled through this portion of the state, and so they are today.

The spire of the old Lutheran church towers against the sky over the town of Walhalla (originally settled by Germans), there is a fine view from Sassafras Mountain farther west, and Lake Keowee near the nuclear plant presents a beautiful panorama surrounded by green hills. Clemson, the location of Clemson University and the John C. Calhoun home, is not far away. Pendleton historic district is nearby and the historic restorations here are excellent.

Greenville is not only an industrial center but the home of Furman University and Bob Jones University. Both institutions are religious in orientation and their graduates are prominent in all areas of South Carolina life.

The capital city of Columbia is a center of culture and education with the University of South Carolina campus, a fine art museum, a zoological park, and examples of historic architecture such as the Robert Mills House. Although most people are familiar with the reputation of the coastal area for beautiful plantation homes, few are aware of the fine ante-bellum houses that still remain in the upcountry between Columbia and Charlotte. The upcountry plantations were smaller but a surprising number may be seen in and near the towns of Camden, York, and Union.

No South Carolinian in his right mind has ever envied a Virginian. He is convinced there is no other state like his own and no state he would rather live in. His state has history, natural beauty, culture, aristocracy, and it has got to have more white columns and more of the character of the Old South than Virginia or Georgia ever thought of having. Why, they even had to come to South Carolina to film much of *Gone with the Wind.*

Many of the descendants of the early settlers from Barbados, England, Ireland, France, Germany, and the northeastern United States are still living in South Carolina. Perhaps they felt they had found a place worth living and worth loving, a place where the climate is mild, where many trees are green the year round. Fall hues of russet, bronze, and gold are subtle and morning mist lies soft upon the fields. There is game to hunt, streams to fish, and a man can be respected and stand tall even if his clothes are a mite threadbare.

The cooler more stimulating climate of the upcountry has, perhaps, lent itself to a faster pace for both agriculture and industry. But there is much to bind the people together, a shared love of horsemanship whether the event is polo in the upcountry or a jousting tournament at Middleton Gardens. The beer-drinking, exuberant crowd at the Darlington Classic stock car race and the people partaking of their elaborate picnic lunch on silver and crystal from the back of their station wagons at the Camden Cup horse race are happy in their own separate worlds. But, they are surprisingly close politically.

In a state where wealth and poverty exist cheek by jowl and tiny shacks are not always far from showplace homes, it is sometimes difficult to find the middle class. They are the merchants and small farmers and if the per capita income is low, one of the reasons is due to larger families.

The rise in per capita income in South Carolina has been more rapid for the past ten years than in the nation as a whole. As industry continues to locate here it will certainly be reflected in an even more substantial rise.

Modern plants, like this one owned by Springs Mills, weave cloth around the clock and, according to one source, 43 per cent of America's broad-woven cotton goods are produced in South Carolina. Despite increasing diversification of industry, textile machinery and apparel still account for the largest portion of the state's manufacturing. And the industry is still growing.

The textile industry has come a long way. The plants are cleaner and quieter. They are air-conditioned and dust and lint is removed immediately.

Although the process of weaving has changed little in the past two thousand years, the machinery has changed. Instead of the old shuttle carrying the yarn, there is a water-jet loom carrying the yarn filler two or three times as fast and much more quietly. Air-jet looms are in the near future.

There are new fibers, new ways of constructing fabrics, and increased study of consumer trends with fabrics produced and sold directly to apparel, home furnishings, and auto industries.

New developments in agriculture and aquaculture pioneered by Clemson University and the University of South Carolina should also result in increased prosperity.

But for the victims of poverty, the state is perhaps the best possible place to be poor, for the soil is fertile enough for most families to enjoy a garden, the climate is temperate, and poverty does not seem to bear down as harshly. Nor is the acquisition of money the all-important goal for most South Carolinians. They are still leisure-oriented and concerned with the quality of life. Business deals are not to be rushed, and there must be time for socializing and interpersonal relations.

It is rare to hear of an old person committing suicide due to loneliness. They have had their place in the community since childhood and with age they are far better able to maintain this position than the elderly who are shunted aside in the life of a busy city. There is still satisfaction in contacts with friends and church and a strong supportive fabric of neighborly concern.

Because South Carolinians have always liked hunting, fishing, horses and the amenities of gracious entertaining, some have concluded that these outdoorsmen are friendly and kind, but not very intellectual. This is a mistake for there have been and are many outstanding men and women from South Carolina in the fields of government and letters.

Henry Middleton and Henry Laurens both served as presidents of the Continental Congress. There was Christopher Gadsden, educated at Bristol England in Latin and Greek, who later became "the firebrand of the Revolution"; John Rutledge, framer of the Constitution and later an associate justice of the U. S. Supreme Court; the "Swamp Fox," Francis Marion, leader of that group of partisan fighters most feared by the British in the low country; Andrew Pickens, the general who helped free the northern part of the state from the British and who was later valued by Washington as a consultant on Indian affairs; Robert Mills, the famous architect who designed the Washington Monument; the LeConte brothers, one a president of the University of California and the other president of the American Association for the Advancement of Science; the Cokers, who were termed leaders in research and farming improvement by the U. S. Department of Agriculture; the Gonzales brothers, nationally recognized in the fields of both journalism and diplomacy; Bernard Baruch, who advised Presidents from Wilson through Roosevelt and later became head of the American Atomic Commission; and James Byrnes, U. S. Secretary of State, Director of the Office of Economic Stabilization, a justice of the U. S. Supreme Court, and an outstanding senator who was known as one of the most influential men in the U. S. Senate.

There was John C. Calhoun, who warned against the centralization of power in the federal government. Senator Robert Y. Haynes, who brilliantly debated Daniel Webster, and one of the greatest leaders of them all, Wade Hampton, who wisely said, "The only way to bring about prosperity in this state is to bring the two races in friendly relation together."

Former South Carolina Reconstruction governor, Daniel Chamberlain, after he returned defeated to his native Massachusetts, wrote:

"It has been remarked that South Carolina has no great leader or leaders after Mr. Calhoun. This was true until 1876, but not later. Great new occasions usually bring leaders. At the head of the Democratic forces in South Carolina, in June, 1876, appeared General Wade Hampton, known only, one might say, till then, except locally, as a distinguished cavalry officer. He had led the life of a planter on a large scale and possessed well-developed powers and habits of command. Totally unlike Calhoun, Hampton's strength of leadership lay not in intellectual or oratorical superiority, but in high and forceful character, perfect courage and devotion to what he conceived to be the welfare of South Carolina. Not even Calhoun's leadership was at any time more absolute, unquestioned, and enthusiastic than Hampton's in 1876; and it was justly so from the Democratic point of view, for he was unselfish, resolute, level-headed and determined. He was for the hour a true natural leader and he led with consummate mingled prudence and aggressiveness."

Chamberlain and the carpetbaggers have been gone for many years, and the ravaged land painfully restored. Modern industrial plants are silhouetted against the sky along the rivers and nuclear plants rise among the hills. Over a hundred thousand newcomers have migrated to South Carolina where twenty years ago the population was predominantly native born. A new spirit is stirring in this state where the majority of the people are young.

From them will rise leaders like those of the past who will also dream great dreams. And, on the far hill, there may be another Wade Hampton with the vision and ability to lead South Carolina to greatness again.

1. Fort Sumpter, Charleston Harbor

2. Carolina Jessamine, the State flower

3. Churchyard wall at St. Helena's in Beaufort

4. (Top left). Boone Hall Plantation at Mount Pleasant

5. (Below). Jousting tournament at Middleton Gardens near Charleston

6. (Top right). The Citadel, Charleston

7. *Yawning leopard, Columbia Zoological Park*

8. *Polar bear at Columbia Zoological Park*

9. *Land's end, Beaufort*

10. *Stoll's Alley, Charleston*

11. *Azaleas in bloom, Cypress Gardens near Charleston*

13. *Old Stone Church on U.S. Highway 76, Pendleton Historic District*

12. *Window on Rainbow Row, Charleston*

14. *Spire of St. Phillip's Church seen through gate of nearby garden, Charleston*

15. Ramey's Mill in the
upcountry

16. Cotton bloom

17. Battery, Charleston

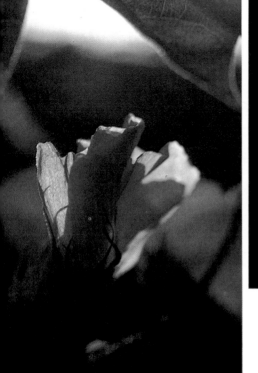

18. *Fishing boats at dusk, Mount Pleasant*

19. *"Catfish Row" from* Porgy and Bess, *Charleston*

SOUTH CAROLINA—
AFTERMATH OF THE "WAR OF
NORTHERN AGGRESSION"

Alistair Cooke, an Englishman, writes in his monumental book on America that thirteen years before secession Lincoln had declared, "Any people, anywhere, being inclined and having the power, have the right to rise up and shake off the existing government, and form a new one that suits them better."

Thus, Lincoln, restating in his own words one of the basic rights of the Declaration of Independence, justified the creation of the Confederate States of America.

Had Lincoln been offered the Presidency of the Confederacy (which would not be so preposterous as it sounds since his southern-born wife lost

On the steps of the capitol in Columbia is this statue of George Washington, his sword broken off by some of Sherman's troops. It was purposely left this way as a reminder.

Only these columns remained to mark the site of General Wade Hampton's home at Columbia after Sherman's troops left.

three brothers in the Confederate Army), the Confederate States of America would be peacefully coexisting as a viable government conducting a relationship with the United States much like our relationship with Canada.

When that brilliant mind died across the street from Ford's Theatre in April of 1865, the hope that South Carolina could escape the vengeance of Radical Republicans, abolitionists, carpetbaggers, and eleven long years of military occupation was gone. With the dawn came the heavy feet of Secretary of War Stanton, President Grant, and Sherman as Commander of the Army in Washington.

Not only had the people of this state fired on Fort Sumter and seceded first from the Union, but there had been a build-up of anger during the acrimonious debates in Congress between John C. Calhoun of South Carolina and Daniel Webster of Massachusetts, home of many of the most violent abolitionists. It was the state the North hated most bitterly.

Each area typified the things that were anathema to the other, and Charleston and Boston were in a sense competitive as each was the "London" of their respective section. Charleston was the center of the plantation economy, its cultural and material eminence based on this as well as its significance as a port city.

Boston was the industrial center for the North and its economy was based on having a supply of cheap raw materials from the agrarian South and the use of child labor (exploitation certainly as morally reprehensible as the institution of slavery, for there was little care or responsibility exercised toward laborers who did not even have a status as "property").

Calhoun was spokesman for the South's agrarian economy and Webster for the industrial economy upon which the development of the North rested. Brilliant as the two men were, they were blind to the faults of the systems of which they were a part. The conflict in economic interest was inescapable and hotheads on each side were unable to adopt a longer view, or compromise for the good of the young nation.

Thus, in no southern state was the destruction by Union troops more devastating and, in spite of the efforts of decent and responsible Union officers, at times more vengeful. On the day General Sherman marched through Winnsboro leaving it in flames, a Union soldier told a Winnsboro physician who stood watching, "There are ten thousand men in this town who would take pleasure in burning every house in it."

After the war, the generals were in control in Washington, and they could hardly forget that this was the home state of Wade Hampton, the general who had conducted many humiliating raids into northern-held territory. A northern traveler in the South after the war wrote that Hampton and Robert E. Lee were the two most loved and influential men in the South.

As the Radical Republican element took over the national government from more moderate men, the desire for vengeance prevailed and during eleven years of occupation federal troops looked the other way while lawless whites and blacks further ravaged the state. The harshness of men like Stanton and Thaddeus Stevens prevailed in Washington and their minions stood on the vanquished sand and red clay of South Carolina like a vengeful elephant.

The beloved officers of the Confederacy came home, some like Hampton, to find their homes destroyed and their families bankrupt. After the early days of Reconstruction they gradually emerged to become leaders. Bitterness existed, but rather than being directed toward the blacks, it was aimed primarily at the carpetbaggers and at Washington.

It was not until over a decade later that Wade Hampton, with the support of eight thousand or more black citizens who could no longer be manipulated, revived the Democratic party and rescued the state from lawlessness, fiscal irresponsibility, and actual thievery in government. Republican governor Daniel Chamberlain was not a bad man, but his associates were a contemptible lot and he was unable to control them. In 1871 "Honest John" Patterson (nicknamed in sarcasm), buying his election to the U. S. Senate, said, "There are five good years of stealing in South

Robert Mills was one of the first Americans trained as an architect. Born in Charleston in 1781, he studied with Thomas Jefferson, later designed the Washington Monument and more than fifty other important buildings, including the United States Post Office, Treasury, and Patent Office buildings in Washington, D.C. This house in Columbia which he designed is now maintained by the Historic Columbia Foundation. Opposite: State capitol building at Columbia.

Carolina yet." Fortunately, he was wrong, for Chamberlain and his slate were defeated in 1876 in what was probably the most exciting election for governor in the history of this country.

After Reconstruction, sons and grandsons inherited something of the high ideals of the ante-bellum era but not always with that generosity and sense of responsibility—perhaps because conditions were so harsh and the land so impoverished. It became a struggle for survival. Gradually, the tolerance of men like Hampton and Petigru was submerged. The trauma of the postwar years was transmitted to the children in such a way that their outlook became based more on inherited emotion than reason.

But beneath everything was an ideal, and, even today, all that is needed is to play "Dixie" in South Carolina to trigger feelings that are still just below the surface.

There is a loyalty here to what Dixie could have been, a subliminal conviction that the Confederacy was the reincarnation of an America without the bureaucracy, and a belief that if we had been the Confederate States of America, we should have reached that ideal of democracy that somehow went wrong when the federal government assumed more power than the state government.

This is what the Southerner feels when he hears "Dixie." He's not putting down the black and he's not withdrawing into the past. He sees the vision he feels Thomas Jefferson and Jefferson Davis saw—the vision briefly held over the banners of the Army of Northern Virginia, for surely no army ever fought so gloriously for an ideal not quite understood, but yet the same ideal that Washington stayed at Valley Forge to seek.

At the close of the Civil War, General Wade Hampton commanded all of General Lee's cavalry forces. After the war, he and Lee were two of the most admired men in the South. (Hampton photo courtesy of University of South Carolina Library)

The wildest statewide election ever held in the United States took place in South Carolina in 1876. On election day, blacks, ushered by carpetbaggers, voted from sunup to sundown in as many precincts as they could get to. In some towns where Democrats had been arrested and imprisoned by Republicans so they couldn't vote, friends from North Carolina and Georgia came across the state line by the hundreds to vote in their place. Even Union officers and soldiers sent to guard the voting places were so sympathetic to Hampton that many slipped into civilian clothes and voted. When it was all over both sides claimed victory. South Carolina was

blessed with two governors and two sets of state legislators separated by a thin line of blue-coated troops who were controlled by the Republican governor but whose sympathies lay with the Democratic governor. Wade Hampton, above, is being carried by his supporters to his inauguration in Columbia. (Sketch from Leslie's Weekly, courtesy of the University of South Carolina Library)

And if it all became lost in some sort of bureaucratic maze in Washington, it is because the true Southerner really knows it all began at Appomattox when the wrong general was forced to surrender. He recognizes that supplies, money, and superior numbers do not insure moral victory.

For the average southern soldier in the Army of Northern Virginia, the issue of slavery was immaterial. Long before the war General Lee had freed the few slaves he had inherited and the wisest southern leaders had been speaking out against slavery for years. By providing cheap labor, slavery had begun to destroy the economic opportunity of many free craftsmen, both white and black.

From 1830 on, there had been increasing anger over laws which favored the industrial North and damaged the agrarian South economically, and the belief that a state had those rights which were not expressly delegated

Wade Hampton was inaugurated in front of Carolina Hall, while at the capitol building federal troops kept Governor Chamberlain in power. To make matters worse, Republicans and Democrats elected their own Speakers of the House, who spoke simultaneously, conducting the affairs of state, while a Union officer sat between them. Virtually every member of these august bodies was armed and neither side would leave the building for fear the other would take over. The dispute was finally ended by Republican President Hayes who picked Democrat Wade Hampton as the rightful governor.

to the federal government. Few South Carolinians would have chosen to die to defend slavery and certainly men like Wade Hampton or Robert E. Lee would not have risked their lives and offered their leadership if slavery were the only issue.

The South Carolinian felt that his duty, although less well-defined, was to oppose slavery of a different sort. He saw the southern states subjugated to a central government, all powerful, without sufficient concern for its individual members. He feared that if States' rights fell, individual rights would fall next. It was, in effect, the original domino theory.

Whether right or wrong, the Southerner fought for it and 40,000 South Carolina soldiers died for that belief.

Aside from the issue of States' rights, the culture of the Northeast and the South were ultimately incompatible. When the collision came it was merciless and cruel, a frontal assault on the very being of the South in the form of brutal military subjugation.

But although its political life and civilization were temporarily destroyed, the culture of the South has never disappeared, for it is bound up with values deeply imbedded in the southern consciousness. Even today there is a unique quality to this culture which continues to evoke sporadic attacks and derision from the North—articles satirizing southern men and women, politicians, accents, and the "good ole country boy," supposedly peculiar only to the South, as well as implications that the South has a corner on poverty and racism not shared by the rest of the nation.

There are still publications overjoyed to exalt any southern writer willing to join their ranks in attempting to prove that there is no justice nor opportunity for the black in the South. A shabby, ludicrous Klan Grand Dragon with a fourth-grade education, speaking for a handful of misfits at a cornfield rally, can find himself prominently reported by the northern press while a thousand voices of intelligence and tolerance, if quoted at all, are relegated to the back pages. A black is shot by a white in Chicago and a similar incident takes place in Atlanta and the headline in the 1975 northern newspaper reads, "Black Murdered in South."

Are slanted editorial versions of events and jibes at the South an indication of something far deeper and more complex in the northern psyche? It would not be surprising to find a profound layer of guilt, of which the "Kick the South" literature may be symptomatic. Surely it would take years to rationalize the killing of 96,000 fellow Americans and a suspicion that the society dealt such a blow had any culture worth serious consideration or

Black and white children paint during a downtown festival on the main street of Columbia. The tables are in almost the same location as the covered wagon in the sketch made on February 6, 1865, when Sherman's troops burned Columbia to the ground. The unfinished capitol can be seen burning at the end of the street.

preservation must by all means be ignored for that could only exacerbate the Northerner's responsibility.

For the past hundred years the "guilt complex" of the South has been aired ad infinitum, but, frankly, it is difficult to find any of this feeling in South Carolina. When the war is mentioned some call it the "Confederate War," others call it the "War of Northern Aggression," and how guilty can you feel about being the victim of aggression? A more revealing study might be the "guilt complex" of the North.

Although there is no question that South Carolina is changing, it carries something of the past along with it. Historic patterns of thinking and feeling seem to survive within us. Thus, many of us participate in a dream. The South Carolinian may think of it as a "way of life." Steinbeck says, "These dreams describe our vague yearnings toward what we wish we were and hope to be—wise, just, compassionate and noble. The fact that we have this dream at all is perhaps an indication of its possibility."

Columbia, photographed from the air at night, appears almost to be in flames again. It was the largest city to be burned to the ground by Sherman. (Atlanta, though smaller, got better press coverage.)

THE GARDENS OF SOUTH CAROLINA

The South Carolinian wrote history on a plot of earth, in pools that resemble curving mirrors, in exotic plants, and in garden walks and terraces. Some of the gardens famous today are a heritage of the golden age of South Carolina's agrarian culture extending from the time of the Revolution to Secession.

Writing of the men of that era, Thomas R. Waring said, "They looked upon life gratefully and found it good. They built good houses, planted fine gardens and cultivated an appreciation of leisure as not incompatible with enterprise and achievement. They respected scholarship, they patronized the arts, they studied statecraft, they practiced oratory, they cultivated manners and, if they produced no notable literature nor music nor painting, they yet drew upon all these for a way of life which, perhaps, in the last analysis, is the greatest of the arts."

Cypress, Middleton, Magnolia, and Brookgreen are the best-known gardens. But there are others—at Orangeburg, Columbia, Sumter, Hartsville and Georgetown. The English novelist, Galsworthy, called Magnolia "the most beautiful garden in all the world." Once a magnificent riverside plantation, it has taken generations of care to produce such elegance.

Dubose Heyward describes the gardens: "The English-planned gardens of Carolina grew and mellowed into gardens unlike any others in the whole world. While today one finds only the broken forest-strewn lines of these first great gardens, their peculiar spirit and charm survive in others created under their influence. . . . and this peculiar quality followed the footsteps of the pioneer as he moved northward and westward across the state."

Middleton is the oldest landscaped garden in America and is said to equal the terraced beauty of Versailles in France. Here stands the awesome Middleton Oak, a thousand years old, with its gnarled trunk thirty-seven feet around. And there are so many different flowers that something is always in bloom and the garden is open the year round.

Many of these gardens are bordered by a river on one side and the forest on the others. They seem to have been wrested from the semitropical forests. Their heart is an open space and around this are masses of azaleas and camellias and arrangements of walks. Many were attempts at formal English gardens but the warm, moist climate produced entirely different results amid the informal, languorous grace of live oaks, Spanish moss, and yellow jessamine vines.

In Charleston even the parking meters are surrounded by beauty.

On this street in McClellanville, South Carolina, the huge live oaks make the cars look like toys.

The sidewalk at Brookgreen Gardens leads to a wonderland of rare plants and statuary.

Cypress Gardens north of Charleston is the most unusual, for it is actually a picturesque cypress swamp turned into a garden. In the midst of the garden enormous azaleas and towering camellias surround the shining black water. Boats wait at the shore to take visitors on a fantastic trip gliding over the dark, mirrorlike water among tall cypresses, under Japanese bridges, and past islands full of flowers. So perfectly reflected in the water are the images of trees and plants that it's an upside-down world evoking memories of Indian tribes that walked into lakes convinced there was a real world beneath the water.

Gardening and the appreciation of beauty are a way of life, and most small towns are a delight to drive through in spring. There are white drifts of dogwood blooms, immense mounds of brilliant azaleas, and trees festooned with lavender wisteria. In Charleston so many flowering shrubs have been planted along the city streets that these shrubs are in bloom from early spring into the summer. Even in the business district, the poorest, most humble Charlestonian may enjoy beauty.

Northward on the coast, the tiny town of McClellanville with less than a thousand people has a haunting charm. The homes are old and weathered and the azaleas profuse and gigantic. The winding streets are named after heroes like Pinckney and Drayton and the town founders, Morrison and Dupre. Ancient oaks make fascinating patterns of sunlight and shadow and

"Diana of the Chase" by
Anna Hyatt Huntington.

On the site of an old rice plantation, Cypress Gardens, now owned by the city of Charleston, affords a dreamlike boat trip drifting through acres of cypress and a profusion of azaleas over hushed lagoons of black water. (Open to the public February 15 through May 1)

one tree so immense and so beautiful that, though it stood squarely in the middle of the road, they simply built the road around it. Elsewhere, it would have been sent crashing earthward and its leafy, primeval corpse hauled away.

Fortunately, the whiteway street light concept never reached McClellanville before the energy crisis, and its tiny business section of three or four stores looks much as it must have looked a half century ago. Sometimes, much may be preserved when "progress" is slow in arriving.

THE PEOPLE OF SOUTH CAROLINA

An event, like a flash of lightning, may illuminate and give an insight into the character of the people who inhabit the land.

Several nights after the battle of Camden where Lord Cornwallis defeated a small, tired American army under Gates, a group of Continental prisoners was being taken to Charleston. After posting a detachment, the British guards bedded down at a plantation house, secure in the knowledge that nowhere in South Carolina was there a company of Continentals left to fight for the American cause.

When, out of the woods at dawn, burst a company of cavalry, and in

a few minutes the sleepy British were overwhelmed, captured, and several hundred American prisoners set free. Francis Marion had arrived leading seventeen men who fought stubbornly on despite the American defeat at Camden. And, for more than a year, the "Swamp Fox" and his men rode out of their lair in the swamps to strike at British outposts, carry off supply wagons, and wreck Tory formations.

Legend has it that a British officer visiting Marion under a flag of truce was invited to share the usual supper of sweet potatoes and water. The young British officer, amazed that men would fight under such conditions, resigned his commission and sailed back to England convinced of the worth of the American cause.

In the paintings of Marion and his company and in the actual records, there is no question that a number of the men who followed him were black, probably making them the first integrated group of soldiers. The tenacity of Marion and others like Pickens and Sumter, their ability to endure hardship and make full use of the resources of the land, were the vital assets against the British.

Joel Poinsett is almost forgotten today except for the fact that he brought the poinsettia plant to South Carolina from Mexico. But he did more than that, for he, too, had considerable military talent. Poinsett was appointed ambassador to Mexico and later Secretary of War. He was sent to Chile as American agent when that country rose against Spain and established a provisional junta in July of 1810. President Madison sent him as consul to determine the stability of the government. Poinsett became friends with the junta leader and convinced him that the most perfect form of government for any people was a democracy. Soon he was engaged in helping Chileans draw up a constitution and encouraging Chile to proclaim its independence.

When the Spanish viceroy in Peru heard of this he immediately launched an invasion of Chile. Poinsett, who had spent seven years in Europe observing military techniques, advised the Chilean leader and helped provision the forces of the new democracy. Direct action again was the favored course.

John and Joseph LeConte were two of South Carolina's most fascinating intellectuals. The brothers, both interested in science, at first opposed secession, but later changed their views and supported the Confederacy. Putting their knowledge of science to work, John, with the rank of major, became head of the Nitre Works in Columbia while Joseph was put in charge of the manufacture of medicine to supply drugs that could not be had by running the blockade. When the harrowing days of the war were past, the brothers decided to go west. There they joined the faculty of the University of California which had just opened its doors and was preparing to receive its first group of students. By 1876, John LeConte was president of the University; he has been called "The Father of the University of California." His brother, Joseph, became one of the founders of the Sierra Club studying the geology and geography of the High Sierra Mountains. In fact, Mount LeConte in California was named for him.

Diverse in nature, tenacious in beliefs, it is hard to find the words to describe the "average" South Carolinian, but most of the people interviewed in this book, as well as Francis Marion, Joel Poinsett, and the LeConte brothers, would agree with the following statement made by Bernard Baruch: "South Carolina is bone of my bone, flesh of my flesh and wherever I may live or whatever I may do, South Carolina is home."

The old home place. Across the red clay upcountry of South Carolina are family homes like this.

WHITE WITCH DOCTOR OF THE
LOW COUNTRY

———◆———

J. E. McTeer of Beaufort, once high sheriff of the low country, probably knows more than any living person about African "root" and witch doctors. In fact, McTeer's knowledge is more than academic, for he became a protégé of one of the most famous witch doctors in South Carolina and his own powers of white magic earned him the grudging respect of the witch doctors of the area.

What is a witch doctor? "We must go back to the days of slavery for an answer," says McTeer. With the slaves came African customs and beliefs. A mere shifting of geographic location made only small differences in their ingrained culture and inner lives. They were Africans, and they adapted to the hot, humid South Carolina low country without really being changed. On the contrary, their culture brought change to the land, introducing a strange and sometimes fearful concept—that of the witch doctor who supposedly had the power to cast spells and influence events for good or evil.

The concept of "root" and the black arts survived the end of slavery and the years that followed.

"I became interested in 'root' from a black couple on my father's farm who were in their eighties—Emmaline and Tony Legare. The fathers of both had been African witch doctors. I heard them discuss spells and potions many times. They would sometimes say when I hung around them too long, 'Boy, we're goin to put the mout on you,' or 'I ga hant you when I dead.' They spoke in the Gullah dialect. At night around the cane boilings, I would listen to them tell of hants, spirits, and evil eyes.

"The witch doctors were firmly entrenched and active when I became sheriff and were involved in many of my dealings with the black and white citizens in my jurisdiction," says McTeer in his fascinating book, *High Sheriff of the Low Country*. "When I became sheriff, the witch doctors in this area were Dr. Buzzard, Dr. Hawk, Dr. Bug, and Dr. Snake; all had fathers who had been witch doctors. They've died out now but I knew them intimately, and they knew I had some force where witchcraft was concerned. We had several confrontations and I made them stop giving medicine orally. They had no right to do this. Dr. Buzzard, who was the most famous witch doctor in America, and I became great friends and he showed me many of his secrets.

The white "witch doctor," J. E. McTeer of Beaufort is holding the caduceus of his profession.

Dr. Eagle, now dead, was once one of the leading witch doctors of Beaufort County. His waiting room, when visited by the writer, was packed with patients of both races from as far as Atlanta.

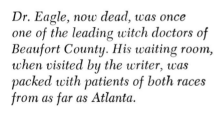

"The true African witchcraft is the oldest witchcraft in the world. When a person comes into my office and tells me they are under the influence of a spirit or spell, I immediately say, 'Yes, you have got a spell on you, I can feel it,' and the chances are I can. 'I can take it off of you. Do you believe I can?' I take possession of his mind and make him know I have the power to take it off him. When I am through, he knows I have taken it off him. I have had the Catholic bishop come with his priests and watch me, and doctors from all over the country.

"I tell a person when he comes here, 'If you pay me it will turn on us both.' I cannot accept anything. Sometimes, they insist on giving me a necktie or something like that but I tell them, 'If you want to do something, send a contribution to one of these groups right here.'" McTeer flipped through acknowledgments from a number of charitable organizations.

What kind of spells do people ask him for? "Everything. 'Make my husband come back to me.' 'Make my husband leave.' 'Kill my husband.' 'I'm sick and there is a spell upon me—help me.' They call me from as far as California with problems that range the gamut of human emotion, but when they believe they are possessed by an evil spirit, I am the only one that can cure them.

"The psychiatrist laughs at them. He tells them, 'You are living in a civilized age; you know that you have no spell on you.' They look at him and say to themselves, 'What a fool you are!'

"I have college professors come, schoolteachers, naval officers, all types. It is pathetic because these are people who believe they are damned unless I can cure them. I have saved five people from suicide in the last six months who would have killed themselves if they had not been able to get that spell off of them. If they don't die, they become paranoid—they believe that some enemy, someone who is jealous of them has put a spell on them."

Are there people in the low country who are still putting spells on people?

"Oh, yes. In fact, I used to put them on too. That's called black witchcraft. But, I gave up the practice of black witchcraft and now I only practice white witchcraft. You ought to see some of the things that happen through black witchcraft, unbelievable!

"A young soldier came to one of the islands not long ago and this witch doctor told him, 'If you go back to camp before the full moon, you'll die.' So, he didn't go back. When he did go back he was AWOL. When the trial came he said, 'I couldn't come back. I wouldn't dare go back. If I came back before the full moon, I'd have died.' 'Why?' asked the officer. 'A spell was put on me,' he replied. So, they court-martialed him and tried him and I wish you could have seen the faces of the colonels and generals as they listened to this tale of witchcraft.

"Now, let me take you back and show you some real witchcraft." We entered a room off the main office and there was an altar with roots and stones and feathers, animal teeth, wax dolls, and various unfamiliar objects.

"This is my emblem of office," he said, picking up a long, grotesquely shaped club. "This was given to me by the witch doctors and denotes my power." He pointed to a figure that resembled a writhing human form. "That's a mandrake. It's what the African witch doctors put their spirits into for evil. As long as it has a gold chain on it, it can do no evil. I remove that gold chain and prepare a root like this one which is a death root and the person will either die or get sick and wish he was dead. That is the animism part of witchcraft—you put your spirit into an inanimate object."

He held a small bag up in his hand. "This is a root I prepare. On the altar there are things living and things dead. Over here is another part of witchcraft, a mamba that came from Egypt. Now, sit down here," and he pointed to the chair in front of him.

"This red hex doll brings you luck and the black is to remove things from you. Now, I must take complete possession of the person's mind. I've convinced him that I have the power to remove the spell and I more or less leave this world, temporarily. Please do what I say. Put your finger down in the bottom of that cup. Now, I am going to take your forces through me into this, put it into an amulet, and that amulet will be part of your life— keep it near you for I will be in it along with your forces.

"Put your finger in this water and put it on your forehead. Place this on your knee," he said handing me a Kleenex he had pulled from a box on the altar. Then he took the Kleenex from me, lit it with a match and touched it to several objects, then placed it in an ashtray where it continued to burn. He took his grotesque emblem and silently pointed it toward the ashtray. I waited. The Kleenex was almost consumed when suddenly it exploded in a flash of light. I examined the ashtray and not even a trace of ash remained!

McTeer's hands fell to his sides and he looked tired. For the first time I was conscious of his age—he is a man in his sixties.

His morning had been a busy one, for a woman had come to him from Augusta referred to him by a doctor there. "She believed she had something live within her body—some people believe they have a frog or a snake or something that they can feel moving. They believe it was put there by black magic. This woman was a highly intelligent, educated person.

"You would be surprised at one lady who came to me, a white college professor. She and this man were teaching together in a psychiatry class. He took a violent dislike to her, so he sent her a picture of herself with her throat cut and the blood running down her dress, saying 'You are under black magic.' She brought me the picture. Since then I've gotten the most beautiful letters from her saying that she is at peace and the professor can have no effect on her anymore. Her life is normal again."

There is no one to inherit the mantle of this white witch doctor. "Charlatans!" he calls the dabblers in witchcraft. "People who have nothing else to do who have run the gamut of life. They want to look into the unknown and they're playing with fire."

Dr. Buzzard, Dr. Eagle, and other famous witch doctors of the area have passed on, but belief in the power of "root" is by no means dead in the South Carolina low country as proved by the following story which appeared in a Kingstree, South Carolina, newspaper on June 7, 1972.

"Prior to the opening of court here Tuesday morning, a man out on bond on four charges of larceny was noticed dusting a powdery substance in front of Solicitor R. Kirk McLeod's desk, Clerk of Court Winnie P. Jones's desk and the chair and desk of presiding Third Circuit Judge Dan F. Laney. Judge Laney immediately ordered the man's bond revoked and he was taken into custody. Bond was reset at $25,000."

Sprinkling root powder to render the evidence harmless and provide the best outcome for the accused used to be far more common than it is today, as was paying the witch doctor to sit in the courtroom and chew root during the trial. This has sometimes so intimidated witnesses that they were unable to testify.

"After the word got around that two famous root doctors had taken me into their confidence and taught me black magic," says McTeer, "I let it be known that I only had the power to 'take the root off' since I am a Christian. Everyone knew that 'putting the root on' is clearly the work of the Devil. I explained that if I accepted pay for doing a Christian's work, the root would turn on me. Seeing men and women relieved of stress and fear, able to be productive and useful again, is my real reward."

PHILOSOPHY OF A
SMALL TOWN EDITOR

———◆———

The manner of the friendly, relaxed man behind the cluttered desk is quiet and low key. His aggressive, sometimes crusading sort of investigative reporting is unusual for a non-daily paper in a small town. Despite the modernistic appearance of the white building that houses his office, Paul League, editor of the Lancaster *News*, shares the traditional values of most South Carolinians. He is a native and has been a journalist for most of his life.

"For sixteen years I was in Seneca on the western tip of the state near the Georgia line. It is smaller than Lancaster. I found that the next day after writing an editorial, I would meet my critics on the street and have to explain my position. There is more directness in a small town and not so much of this false façade. Although they speak what they think, when the chips are down or when you're in trouble they come to your aid. In a larger area they couldn't care less. You've heard this many times but it's true."

Are the small South Carolina towns being bypassed for the cities?

"I don't think so," says League. "Can you really say that this state has anything but small towns, outside of Greenville, Columbia, and Charleston?

"The people in our small towns tend to stay put. They have carved out their place. They have either achieved a reputation for eccentricity or for their good deeds. The closeness has much to recommend it. I prefer living in a small town. I've newspapered in Charlotte and on other daily papers but a small town is where I'd like to raise my children and did raise them."

Do they get all the intellectual stimuli they need in a small town? League chuckled. "Well, I don't know that they get all that, but you see, you're talking with a small town editor who has old-fashioned values. You have so much closer supervision over your children. They can't do too much before people begin to know about it. There is a good amount of tolerance but when your children get too far out of line, there is concern and you usually hear about what has happened rather than waking up to it too late.

"In the small town itself, you know there's a black living here and a white living there. It's not segregated. People are pretty mixed as to both race and income level and they tend to know and understand each other better. Small towns want to grow and become larger but this opportunity to know each other is the town's greatest asset. It would be a shame to lose this.

"When I was editor of the Seneca paper, a cute thing happened. At graduation time I wrote an editorial which said, 'Instead of going out and painting the water tower with your initials and raising hell graduation night, do something worthwhile that will let your class live on in memory, plant a tree.' I wrote it, tossed it in the bin and forgot about it. I had a daughter who graduated that year, and the morning after graduation I got up, pulled the curtain back at the window and looked out. Then I did a double take. In the middle of my lawn was a huge tree that had not been there the day before. It was propped up with fieldstone and fence posts. It took a lot of doing but those young people had planted a tree! They knew the editor of the paper and where he lived. In a city most people have no idea where the editor of the paper lives, right?

"I think it's healthy because we are rubbing elbows every day and we're communicating. In a large town you don't know whether you are or not.

"Our communities retain a lot of the virtues and standards of the past. Every town is built up around its church. That's the social center and this goes back to the old days when there was nothing else. We still have the church picnics and in-gatherings when everyone comes back to their home church and I think they still have a tremendous impact on a small community.

"Certain individuals also exert considerable influence—the school principal, the family doctor, the leading-citizen type.

"Some of the towns are dying while others grow because of their proximity to a city, like Winnsboro to Columbia. They sprang up with the railroads. Then the little textile mill was started in almost every town and this was what provided the major employment other than farming. Now this is changing. They are closing down the old, dilapidated brick piles that used to be textile plants where the guy went in at six o'clock in the morning and came out at six o'clock in the afternoon. The question is what is going to happen?

"The answer will come as the state locates non-polluting light industry for these towns. Greenville and Spartanburg and Columbia can take care of themselves and they have their own people out securing industry. The state will have to take inventory and say, look, the mill in this town is closing and we have X number of people here that can work and they are good workers, the best workers in America today, for they are people who are going to give a dollar's worth of work for every dollar they get.

"They are not going to be absent every Monday like some of the workers on an assembly line in other parts of the country where they may have to shut down a production line because not enough workers show up to operate it. The work ethic here comes from the Bible background. Our founding fathers held similar principles.

*Small-town newspaper
editor, Paul League.*

"The small town has a cohesiveness and elicits a loyalty that is seldom present in a larger place. You say something about Lancaster and my managing editor who is a native, man, he gets up on his hind legs and defends it. This is his home. He believes in it and there's no other place, no better place. I like that. In a city you have people who perhaps haven't had a home in a long time or maybe it's home for only a short while before they move on. They don't have time to identify with it.

"In some towns there is an outstanding individual who takes the community under his wing and feels a responsibility to take care of it. Here in Lancaster it was Colonel Springs. About 60 per cent of our teachers here have their master's degrees. The Springs Foundation has paid the full cost for the teacher to get her master's. You see this is a small-town concept. Colonel Springs had a heart and saw to it that his people came first. He recognized their loyalty to him and he in turn had a loyalty to them. He provided so much for these people—perhaps hurt them in a sense—because when it is time for them to give themselves things, say raising taxes to improve schools or build an auditorium, they look around to see where Colonel Springs is and they don't make the effort. I'm saying this is a possibility.

"Of course, there is a difference in towns. Some are dominated by a few families. They own all the property uptown and they control the pace of progress. You've heard the saying, 'If we had about five good funerals we could do this or that.' But meantime they can't. They are losing population and the downtown is dead. The people themselves are pretty content. You need diversified industry; you need little theater, the arts, and some recreational facilities if you are to keep your young people.

"Lancaster is on the move. The leadership here is impressive. It is young, aggressive and, I think, trying to plan for orderly growth."

Dogwoods bloom in downtown Abbeville, South Carolina, a typical South Carolina small town.

SHE SAVED THE CHARLESTON
SKYLINE

———◆———

Nancy Stevenson's most dramatic battle was fought before she became a representative to the state legislature. Mrs. Stevenson led the resistance against a high-rise building project that Charlestonians felt was entirely out of keeping with the architecture of their city.

"Charleston is a city built on both a human scale and a humane scale. When you walk down the street, you are not overpowered by tall buildings. There are trees and gardens. You live in a city designed for people and I hope we can maintain that scale.

"We had great good fortune in the form of an editorial and picture which appeared in the Washington *Post* on the SAVE CHARLESTON campaign.

Legislator Nancy Stevenson at the gate to her home.

Citadel cadets march out of the barracks for their Friday afternoon parade.

Citadel cadet on parade.

Citadel cadet after the parade with his girlfriend.

One of Charleston's famous flower
ladies selling Christmas wreaths to
passing motorists.

At the Battery in Charleston where
carriages and horses wait for tourists,
these two horses seem to be
exchanging a bit of friendly gossip.

Rush-hour traffic across the Ashley River Bridge.

Dusk falls on Charleston. The gaslights begin to glow along the streets and, in the interval before darkness and the harsh glare of the electric lights, the past lives briefly.

It must have been widely read for we received contributions from all fifty states and from ten foreign countries—even Israel in the middle of the war.

"Twenty-five per cent of the contributions came from people who had never seen Charleston but they were so disgusted and fed up with what developers had done to their towns that for them the contribution was a protest against big money interests coming and destroying what people hold dear. Their letters would say 'Don't let the developers do to your town what they did to ours.' With the help of these contributions we were able to raise the money to buy the property and block the high-rise.

"The most desirable step would be zoning legislation limiting the height of high-rise buildings to some landmark. Unfortunately, we have people who consider growth in terms of feet in the air. I think they must have

Polished brass knobs and other ornate details decorate town house entrances. How many hands have rested upon this knob?

Gates are everywhere in Charleston.

Through the passage beyond the gate is an interior, private world.

their feet planted in the air, for the very qualities tourists come here to see are those that these people would obliterate so that Charleston would soon resemble any other city. It would seem that the tourist trade, alone, would be sufficient for our business interests to zealously guard and back historic preservation here, for it is the unique atmosphere of the past that draws our tourists."

Nancy Stevenson is finding new challenges for her abilities in the state legislature. She is particularly disturbed by cuts in the education budget.

"We are graduating functional illiterates from our high schools. Somehow, our priorities have gotten mixed up. We put a considerable portion of our budget into higher education and I'm certainly not against higher education. But hundreds of our children graduate from high school and are not even equipped to pass the tests to take trade-school programs offered by the unions, much less go to college.

"I think the first thing that we must do is reduce the teacher-pupil ratio in the lower grades. I don't care how good a teacher is. She cannot teach thirty-five or forty children to read in forty-five minutes a day. It's impossible. It should be a maximum of one to twenty, preferably one to fifteen or eighteen. Then you have a chance of teaching the children to read. I would like to see two years of mandatory kindergarten and a teacher-pupil ratio of one to twenty in the first three grades. By the fourth grade, I think every student would read on a fourth-grade level and could then begin to learn history, social studies and be capable of reading word problems in math.

"A child that hits the fourth or fifth grade and cannot read on that level gets frustrated and falls further and further behind, becoming a disruptive influence and perhaps ultimately a delinquent. We have a lower teacher-pupil ratio in our high schools than in our grammar schools. It doesn't make sense.

"We are starting a second medical school and we can't afford it. We are a poor state. The idealistic thrust behind this is to get more doctors into the rural areas and I know this need exists. But I don't care how many doctors you produce, they are not going into the rural areas unless better facilities are built for them in these areas and they receive some extra emolument from the state.

"At Annapolis, for example, your education is paid for and then you have to sign a contract to stay in the Navy for five years. Conceivably something of this sort might be tried with our medical schools. You go for free, you may even get paid a small sum upon graduation, and you sign a contract that you will go to a rural area for three years. We need to try new and feasible approaches.

"I think there will be a reversal of the trend of people leaving our small towns for the cities. It is already happening where new industries have located in rural areas. Among young couples the appreciation of the kind of life you can have in a small town is far greater than it was in my genera-

Wrought-iron work was as beautiful as any in England. The sword gate on Legare Street is a masterpiece.

St. Philip's Church as seen through the gate to the cemetery. Many great South Carolinians are buried here including John C. Calhoun.

There are still a few cobblestone streets left in Charleston.

tion. But there must be enough jobs for our young people to stay there and make a living."

Mrs. Stevenson does not find being one of the few women in the legislature a disadvantage. "My husband was in the legislature fifteen years ago and some of the men he knew are still there. Perhaps that helped some, the men have been very cordial. When I was running for the legislature, one of my opponents said, 'She won't be able to go into the smoke-filled rooms where the men sit around in their undershirts.' South Carolina legislators don't sit around in their undershirts and I haven't been kept out of any smoke-filled rooms."

A rose blooms in the cemetery across the street from St. Philip's Episcopal Church.

WE SHARE THE LAND TOGETHER

———◆———

Some call Jim French a militant. Editor of a three-year-old weekly newspaper for blacks, French is a tall, light-skinned man on the young side of forty.

The *Chronicle*'s bright gold letters and neatly kept building stand out in sharp contrast to most of the shabby storefronts on King Street, the shopping area for several thousand Charleston blacks. The paper's receptionist-secretary is an intelligent young woman who screens visitors on the street side of an impressive, black-cushioned door to the inner sanctum.

There is another touch of the dramatic in French's office, with its glowing red carpet and low lighting. The room is comfortable and informal with large easy chairs. On a file cabinet near his desk rests an assortment of camera equipment, for between writing editorials and news stories, he functions as staff photographer.

Although he was born in the same state as a man called John Brown, it is hard to find any real traces of fanaticism, for French talks like a pragmatist. He believes that blacks and whites are in the same boat which can be sunk if both races are not willing to work together.

Jim French spent twenty years in the Navy. "I was stationed here in Charleston for two years and I had been all over the country when I decided to come here to settle down and raise a family. I went around the world twice and was stationed in New York, Philadelphia, Baltimore, New London, Connecticut, and Boston, but I wanted to be away from the big city atmosphere. Charleston combines the advantages of a smaller place and a city and you don't have the pollution and traffic problems.

"Crime is not really bad in comparison to other cities the same size. Most of the crimes you read about in the daily press are committed by blacks but that's not the whole story. Many crimes in the better white families —sons who have gotten busted for drugs or assault on a young woman— never make the papers.

"The *Chronicle* has been accused of being antiestablishment. When we report a case of police brutality, we don't report the police version—we leave that to the daily press—we report the victim's version of what happened."

French does not think that police brutality in Charleston is widespread. "We have maybe three cases a year of outright police brutality. I think we have a unique position here in that we can benefit by the mistakes of

James French, editor of Charleston weekly newspaper.

other southern cities. We've never had any major black-white confrontations such as riots. We've had strikes, like the hospital and sanitation strikes, but no fighting, violence, and burning. We're slowly reaching that point, but I think it can still be turned around.

"We have people from the outside who have relocated here. They've left Philadelphia or Detroit because of plant shutdowns and they come South. It's gotten too hot up there for the drug pushers. In New York they throw you in jail and throw the key away for drug pushing. Here you have drugs flowing in through the seaports, and drugs flourish in this state, particularly, in the Beaufort County area.

"You can go to any black housing project and see the big cars—New York, upstate Maryland. They're here for one reason—they've been run out elsewhere and they've come here to sell drugs. Authorities are aware but they don't have either the manpower or help they need and I blame the taxpayers for not making these resources available to local authorities. People don't want taxes raised. They buy police dogs and get new locks and bars on the windows. Eventually, even that doesn't work.

"We are going to have to make our laws more strict. I think a conviction for selling drugs should be a mandatory sentence the same as using

71

a gun to kill someone. We have too many of these people returning to do the same thing.

"Another thing we try to editorialize on is education to increase employment. The job situation for blacks here in Charleston is not as good as it might be, but I think if you want to work and have some qualifications, you can find a job here. We don't depend on just one or two large industries for survival. We have the military, the tourist business is improving each year, and we have the medical complex which absorbs quite a bit of the black population. I think the blacks are taking advantage of the training because when I go out there I see blacks all over the place.

"Our middle-class blacks are probably being hurt more by inflation than any other group. They are heavily in debt and mortgaged and jobs are harder for them to find, while they are trying to live like the middle class is supposed to live. There just don't seem to be enough jobs for this group, and some of them seek out government programs.

"We are antihandout from the government or anybody else. We have people in various government-funded programs and they get millions of dollars to help the poor people. Unfortunately, some of them use it to provide a salary base for their middle-class friends. We are totally against this and we discuss it all the time. I'm for Head Start and certain other programs that train people, but I am against subsidizing laziness and that is what we are too often doing.

"I talked to a lady the other day who says she receives a welfare check from North Carolina. Her mother lives there, receives her check once a month and forwards it to her, but she lives here. Here she goes down and gets food stamps. She works at a restaurant four hours a night 'just to be doing something.' She says she doesn't have to work and she lives a good life. She brags about this. It bothers me. And she is no isolated case. I know people around here who get food stamps, whites and blacks, and sell them. They don't need them.

"The best kind of help we can give people would be vocational education and the opportunity to get a job—just the opportunity. Don't give me anything I'm not going to work for. I don't want it. We got too many people who survive with their hands out and they do very well, thanks to the government.

"The biggest challenge I think I have with this paper is the hope I have of changing the attitude of people, both whites and blacks. I think in this town we have a very unique situation. Blacks and whites respect and love each other. They live next door to each other. We have no rooted black community. There is one part of town, the east side, that is all black but everywhere else, it's all integrated, so we've made the first step. In fact, it's always been that way. It's not like the North where you have the black side of town.

"I'm afraid that the politicians and those who are in a position to bring about change will wait until we have a problem before they decide what to do. I'm saying to the city officials, we can see we have a beautiful town, why don't we take steps now to weed out those people who are coming here just to start trouble between blacks and whites?

"We have organizations who just want to start a hassle. Mostly they are out-of-state people, but they have recruited young people who have no roots whatever. They listen to the propaganda. They attend meetings and they are just waiting for some cop to abuse them—a black person—to raise hell. They're waiting to find a crusade.

"The black separatist attitude hasn't come to Charleston yet. I think we need to maintain our identity as black people, our heritage, our culture, but we still have to live together as people.

"I'm always hearing of people coming here who just got back from New York, 'just couldn't take it no more.' They come in and say, 'Help me find a job, get some information.' Blacks have returned because we just don't have the hostility down here. You go to Boston, you got hostility." He smiled at his understatement. "We have isolated instances in the South, we all know that, but I'm talking generally."

Jim French is sold on education. "I went to college for two years and then didn't have the money to go on so I went in the service. That's where I got the rest of my education and I can thank them for that. I don't say we have an adequate educational system; we don't have. But part of that is money and that problem exists all over the state. Inner-city schools here are all black by legislation and we're trying to change that. In North Charleston the schools are integrated. In the past we've had quite a few cases of violence in the schools, particularly the black schools. Shootings among the students, blacks shooting blacks, most of the time. Students who came on the campus or some little hood who started raising hell somewhere and it ended up at the school. The administration of these inner-city schools is all white and while we have some black input, I think we need more in the decision-making body. It's basically all white thinking. In the integrated schools the problems are there but not the shootings.

"We went out and did a series of interviews with both races in the integrated schools. The white kids would say, 'If you have any problems downtown it's for one reason. You have segregated schools. These are not blacks saying this but white class presidents and leaders. They also say, 'If you have a father on city council or other positions in the city, the money is going to go to the integrated schools their kids go to.' That's just politics—the way it works. Meanwhile the inner-city schools crumble.

"But, I guess the biggest thing the *Chronicle* is trying to push is equality. We don't push a black because he's black. We don't say give a guy a job to meet your quota because he's black but hire him if he's qualified —it's equality of opportunity. Give him a chance."

SHE MAKES THE POTTERY OF
HER ANCESTORS

◆

Not far from where Andrew Jackson played as a boy is a place on the wide and winding Catawba River known as Nation's Ford. For centuries the people of the Catawba Indian Nation crossed here between the two Carolinas. Washington, and later Cornwallis, forded these shallow waters. The southern banks of the river were the home of a powerful people, the Catawbas, one of the few Indian tribes that always befriended the white settlers.

The once mighty Catawba Nation has now dwindled to only about twelve hundred people, most of them living near the reservation a short distance from Rock Hill or in other upcountry towns and cities.

Mrs. Fox Ayers of Columbia, a dark-haired, shy woman, is one of the few who are still able to make the traditional Catawba pottery. A highly skilled potter, Sarah Ayers learned the art as a child. She has demonstrated her pottery making at craftsmen's gatherings as far away as Connecticut and Ohio and in several museums.

"I get my clay from the same place our people have always found it, near the river. My husband's grandmother used to dig her clay right where I do now. We have been making this pottery for two hundred years or more, for as long as our tribe has lived near the river. The Catawbas often traded their pottery with the early settlers for food or clothing or whatever they wanted," says Mrs. Ayers.

Most of her pottery follows the traditional designs for the making of cook pots, water pitchers, bowls, canoe-shaped trays, and peace-pipe holders.

"In the early days these were used for cooking," she says as she molds a three-legged pot. "The handles are shaped like war bonnets. When I go to the river I dig two kinds of clay, one with the consistency of putty and the other a sandy-type clay. Then I blend them together. The blended clay is for my pots and pitchers. The putty clay is just right for making pipes. My colors come out in the firing and range from beige to black and red."

Most of the pottery was utilitarian but the Catawbas also made some for their own pleasure and for decoration. Just as her ancestors did, Mrs. Ayers sometimes shapes birds, turtles, frogs, beavers, and ducks.

"I don't glaze my pottery," she says. "After it is dry, I take a cloth and wet it, then rub it over the pottery. After that I take this smooth stone from the river bottom and pass it over the pottery many times until the piece

Sarah Ayers makes the Catawba pottery of her ancestors.

A shell is used to smooth the coils.

A display of Catawba Indian pottery made by Sarah Ayers. In the background is the Catawba River along which the Indians lived for generations. The source of their clay for pottery is near the river.

begins to shine." She fondled some of her polishing stones thoughtfully. One was a deep amber and gleamed like satin. "These were left to me by my grandmother who used them herself over fifty years ago."

The Catawbas never used a wheel in making their pottery but rather made long snakelike coils and built them up layer upon layer into a pot or a bowl or a pitcher. "After I add a few coils I must wait for them to dry before placing more on top, or the weight would pull the piece out of shape. While it is still damp I use a mussel shell to smooth over the coils."

Catawba pottery is baked in an open fire. Three successive fires are made and each is allowed to burn down to the coals before the pottery is judged to be ready. The Catawbas have never used kilns. Mrs. Ayers likes to temper her pottery first in her own oven gradually raising the temperature to 550 degrees. "After I have allowed the third fire to burn down, I cover my pottery completely with wood chips and that is the secret of giving it the various colors.

"I have always loved making my pottery. When you don't feel like doing anything else you can sit down and start something. You'll begin to think about that piece until your mind becomes your hands and your hands become your mind and everything runs together as you watch, like someone standing far off, to see what it will turn out like. Everything in you is working real hard to see that it comes out right and you can't think about anything else.

"If you make a piece you particularly like you want to go right back and try another. Sometimes, as I work, I wonder about my people making their pottery this way a hundred years ago and whether some woman like me took the same pride in it and whether she polished and finished it as carefully as I do today." Mrs. Ayers' dark eyes were far away as she passed her fingers thoughtfully over a beautiful black-and-beige pot.

"You know, I had quite a surprise when I visited the Museum of the American Indian in New York. I was there to study artifacts and pottery when suddenly I saw a piece that looked so much like Catawba pottery I stopped to look at it more closely. The name on the card said 'Sarah Harris' —that's my name you know, Sarah Harris Ayers—and I found it had been made by my own grandmother and purchased on the Catawba Reservation years ago.

"When you make a piece of pottery something of yourself goes on and on, doesn't it?"

Mrs. Ayers' pottery has already received wide recognition among museum people and collectors and, undoubtedly, something of herself will go on and on.

A DECENDANT OF THE MAN
WHO SHOOK LAFAYETTE'S HAND

◆

He is the great-great-great nephew of a man who knew Lafayette, a man who shook his hand at Charleston. And here he is today living among those same red clay hills in the upcountry that his ancestor knew and loved. A respected, successful businessman and civic leader, he muses about his state and Fairfield County.

"I think South Carolinians are more like Virginians. They are people of sentiment with ties to the land. Many descendants of our old families have stayed here," says F. Creighton McMaster of Winnsboro.

"Everything used to be cotton but cotton gradually destroyed the soil. Roosevelt's conservation policies helped change that. In many sections of South Carolina the paper companies acquired tremendous lands. Our economy is now more mercantile and industrial with far fewer people deriving a living from the land.

"We had voluntary integration of some of our schools here in the county, then the court ruled, no all-black schools. There were two integrated and four black. When we followed the court and mixed the schools, the blacks were in the majority and many whites pulled out. The best white leadership has had moments of discouragement. Some young blacks are distrustful and we need to work for good will and a more co-operative relationship. Some of our teachers are no longer able to cope with the problems that have arisen through integration. They have left teaching or joined the staff of an academy.

"We like the blacks and we want them to have equal opportunities. I've sometimes felt that up North they liked them as long as they were at a distance. They don't have the good memories we have."

F. Creighton McMaster who is the owner of the Winnsboro Petroleum Company wears conservative business suits and is such a quiet-voiced, courteous man that sometimes the thoughts he expresses are a surprise. Like most South Carolinians he has been steeped in the history of his area since childhood.

"I remember my grandmother talking about Reconstruction. The North put their foot on our neck economically, and this has been a factor in our recovery after the war. I've always felt Southerners make better soldiers. Ain't but one way to fight and that's to fight. We're fiery down here. I've gone in fighting knowing I was going to get hell beaten out of me. I'd fight for principle's sake even if I knew I was going to lose.

"Some Yankees are cold people. As a rule they are cold-blooded businessmen. They're money, money, money. Our business relationships with many northern firms are cold relationships. I like to do business where there's a human element. If I had to foreclose on a man, I'd go out and talk with him, try to soften the blow, see how I could help him. But with a Yankee, that's it!"

F. Creighton McMaster of Winnsboro.

THE ZOO DESIGNED BY ANIMALS

"Animals should design a zoo, not people," says John Mehrtens, director of the unusual Zoological Park at Columbia, South Carolina.

"We are just beginning to learn the effect the environment of a building can have on people. I think it can be vital to the physical and emotional health of animals. It enrages me to think of what many non-professional zoos do to animals when they house them inadequately. I would like to see the staff of some of those zoos in such facilities. Feeding and cleaning their quarters regularly would not be enough. The lack of privacy, stimuli, and exercise would destroy a person and some fine animals are being destroyed that way.

"The first criteria for good design in a zoological park is to intimately understand the physical and psychological requirements of the species you are going to house. You take a basic knowledge of the animal and combine it with careful study of his native home.

John Mehrtens.

Giraffes at the Columbia Zoological Park.

A sleeping lion at the Columbia Zoological Park.

A kangaroo getting a drink of water at the Columbia Zoological Park.

A polar bear sniffing visitors at the Columbia Zoological Park—and deciding they don't smell like Eskimos.

"You can't properly exhibit a tiger unless you are familiar with how he lives in his own land. How does he function in his own environment? What do you know about his mind? Does he like to live alone, in a family unit, or as part of a tribe? How aggressive does he become at mating time and is he a threat to other animals? How much space does he normally roam and what sort of compromise can be made without stressing him? How great a proportion of his environment should consist of plants?

"The next step is to take these factors and combine them with the practicality of caring for the animal. The keeper has to clean the facility, feed the animal, control the animal. The animals must be put in a position where they can be closely observed, medicated, treated. This involves hot and cold water, special paint, smooth concretes as opposed to rough, drop bolts on the switch doors, animal chutes, et cetera.

"The exhibits themselves were built from scale models developed from a series of photographs from the animal's habitat. All of the work was contracted to various companies with the exception of specialized things like the cork trees made by our own Art and Exhibits Department."

Considering the needs of each animal with the architect, you then attempt to turn these special environments into a structural reality—the blueprint. "You take this blueprint, give it to a contractor and go completely bananas because the typical contractor is used to building rectangular ranch houses with no unusual aspects. No one has ever taught him how to string wire mesh on a cage. On a catch cage they simply don't know how to pull it tight and if it's loose, it could hurt the animal.

"You combine all of these factors and then try to visualize it from the viewpoint of the lay public who have no idea what a Siberian tiger is, the biotope (environment) and biome (microenvironment within the environment). You say to yourself, if I were a typically biologically illiterate lay person and I looked at this exhibit, what could I learn from it?

"Thus, you produce a controlled exhibit that reflects the animal in its environment. You don't allow the public to feed the animals because animals in the wild aren't fed by people. You don't exhibit the animal in such a way that he will be stressed by people.

"Somewhere along in there you have to figure out things like jump lines, how far the animal can jump from a sit, how far the animal can jump from a run, how high he can jump vertically. It is important to figure these factors so that you can allow the animal the maximum freedom in his environment and insure safety for human visitors. Is the animal a carom jumper or is he a straight jumper? Is he afraid of height? If he is an animal that is frightened of moving water, no fence will be needed.

"Our monkeys on the island could easily jump twenty or thirty feet across the water and would do so if it were not moving. The water is just a psychological barrier. How does the animal react to light level? Our exotic birds have no glass or wire separating them from visitors. But the light level

A sea lion takes his afternoon siesta.

Playful sea lions at the best zoo in the South.

in the rain forest where the birds live is much brighter than the light level of the visitor's walkway, so they stay in the rain forest."

The birds feel at home in the strikingly realistic tropical forest where there is a torrential rainstorm twice a day. The rainstorm is a bit of computer magic ingeniously programmed to unleash recorded thunder and flashes of simulated lightning along with swelling rainfall which sends the birds flitting for dry nooks under ledges until the storm dies away in the distance.

Other Mehrtens innovations are the large plate-glass windows below water level to allow viewers to watch the gigantic polar bears frolic in their 90,000-gallon filtered pool. An unusual feature of the large cat and bear grottos is the closed-circuit television allowing humans to watch the animals care for their young in the cubbing dens.

The housing for the apes is all beneath the rock islands so they can go inside and enjoy family housing, with individual units for each animal where a baby can be born. The apartments are all heated and air-conditioned, and they are equipped with soundproof cubbing dens.

"When we take care of the needs of the adult animals, we find they take better care of their young," says Mehrtens.

John Mehrtens is a New Yorker in his forties who has more than twenty years experience in curatorial jobs at zoos in Ohio, Fort Worth and Victoria, Texas.

"I decided to be a 'zoo man' when I was six. I had never seen a zoo at that time, but my father killed a caterpillar on his tomato plants which bent me out of shape because this was a very beautiful thing and I couldn't understand why he killed it. When I was eight, or thereabouts, in New York City, you could get a library card and I read a book on caterpillars and found out they turned into butterflies and this was fascinating. When I was ten I belonged to two nature clubs, started to keep my own animal collection at home, and went to zoos every weekend and bugged hell out of the keepers.

"At New York University I majored in biology and found out nobody wanted to hire people to work in zoos. I went to work for a company as an office manager but at home I kept building up my own collection of exotic reptiles, small mammals, and birds.

"One weekend I was lonely for a kindred spirit so I got in the car and drove to a zoo several hundred miles away. In the course of the conversation the director said, 'You know, I need a reptile man.' 'Sold,' I replied. That was twenty-three years ago.

"One policy I have always been opposed to is the hand-rearing of any animals. We totally disagree with the concept of animal nurseries where an animal is taken from the mother and raised by humans. We want tigers that function as tigers; we do not want a tiger or any other animal that is imprinted on by humans and, thus, does not function well socially with its own species.

"We continue importing more animals for the zoo and sixteen additional giraffes arrive soon from Africa. It has taken three long years to get them because of federal regulations which seem to tie up everything including giraffes. (I would like to make a comment in the office in private about federal regulations.)

"I personally feel that a Zoological Park is similar to an art museum, virtually identical except in one way. An art museum serves as a repository for the masterpieces of mankind. It is a cultural enrichment of the human mind. A zoological park is exactly the same. It serves as a repository for the masterpieces of nature.

"When the last tiger ceases to walk as a wild creature, it would take another creation, another universe, another four billion years of evolution to produce that animal again. Once man destroys any given species he cannot recreate it and, thus, I feel the zoological park has a critical role in the enlightenment of man," says John Mehrtens.

"Much of the world's natural habitat is being destroyed. Experts have predicted the total destruction of the world's rain forests within fifty years. The polar regions are rapidly becoming contaminated and Jacques Cousteau has predicted that the oceans of the world will die within twenty years, unless immediate changes occur. The zoological park in maintaining reproductive groups of birds and mammals may become the ark of a world where many creatures are doomed due to the bruising foot of man."

WHERE A GROUND HOG CARRIES
THE MAIL

◆

"When I retired from the textile mill in Anderson in '53, I told my wife, 'I'm going back to the mountains where I was raised and find me a place where it's so rough a ground hog has to carry the mail.' I found this place and when I saw that shoal right there in the stream, I said to myself, I can get enough fall to put me up a mill. I had about ten foot and I built a dam so it would pour on the top of the wheel.

"I built the whole thing myself except for that wheel and I got my son-in-law who runs a machine shop to make me a water wheel. I built the support for that wheel on solid rock, then connected it and got it going just like I wanted it. At the textile mill I worked in all kinds of machinery, and I'd run a corn mill off and on all my life."

R. N. Ramey was sixty-three years old when he built his mill in the mountains not far from Clemson. Now he is eighty-five but on Monday,

Mr. R. N. Ramey.

The mill that Ramey built.

The water wheel at Ramey's mill.

Wednesday, and Friday, he grinds grain into flour from early morning until dusk.

"They come to my mill from everywhere. From Anderson, Greenville, and Spartanburg and I'm getting too old for this but I like it too much to quit.

"Before I got my cats I'd grind a sack of meal and the first night the rats would get into it. Now, I can leave it a month. My four cats follow me everywhere I go, to the house and out into the woods. I take 'em something to eat every morning. They're the smartest cats I've ever seen. The rats don't bother nothin'.

"And I've got an ole dog here, an ole bobtail dog. I got him at the pound. I had the biggest rats; I'd never seen rats that big and long. They'd fight a cat—great big ole brown rats—and this ole dog cleaned them up. They was a whole bunch of 'em over at the mill. I could see their holes where they'd stay in the ground and that dog destroyed every one of them. And moles, he'd scratch them right out. Last winter he killed three possums and dragged 'em up to the house.

"Everybody wants to know who will run the mill when I'm gone. My sons aren't interested. They all have their own jobs. They've always made big money working in the cotton mill. Young people don't want to fool with such as this. It takes an old man to run a mill. Young people can't stay in one place long enough.

"There was a crowd come from Clemson about a year ago and asked me if I cared for 'em coming in and looking. I told them no, I didn't mind. They was all decked-out fellows—good education, and I ain't got no education. I can read and write, that's all. I just went through the third grade.

"One of them looked at the mill and said, 'Mr. Ramey, who'd you get to engineer this job for you? I thought they was makin' fun of me. I said, nobody. I done it myself, just with main strength and awkwardness. He said, 'Well, you've done a damn good job of it.'"

BRANCHVILLE, U.S.A.

———◆———

In the late afternoon sunlight driving up Highway 21, the flat farmland looked little touched by history or time. Who would know driving across the railroad tracks that anything of particular importance had ever occurred at Branchville? There was a small battle there. Confederate troops burned the bridge and turned Union troops around toward Orangeburg, yet something intriguing had happened at this small town.

As the railroad was being laid down from Charleston to Hamburg, South Carolina, in 1833, it went through Branchville, the longest stretch of railroad tracks in the world. Then, right there in the middle of Branchville, they split those tracks and for the first time a pair of railroad tracks gave birth to another pair of railroad tracks. And from that first splitting, like the first division of a cell, the railroad tracks multiplied and multiplied again

The Branchville Railroad Station where three Presidents stopped to eat.

until they connected every hamlet and village in the United States with a web of shining steel rails.

And between the tracks in that little railroad restaurant more Presidents of the United States stopped and dined than at any other place in South Carolina. McKinley, Theodore Roosevelt, Howard Taft, all ate in the surprisingly elaborate restaurant there. Next time you see a railroad, remember that no one knows where all the tracks go, but ultimately if you follow them back to their beginning, they came from Branchville.

The first branch railroad in the United States is right here where, for the first time, the rails split off in different directions.

THE WHEAT OF THE FUTURE

Robert R. Coker, president of Coker's Pedigreed Seed Company, believes that his new variety of wheat will go far in helping to feed a hungry world.

"Look at the large grains," says Coker proudly holding it. "These strong, short stalks support the heavy bearing heads and the uniform height of this wheat makes a field of it a delight to the eye." The new wheat will be ready for farmers in 1976.

The Cokers of Hartsville have long been agricultural pioneers, and for over half a century have had a revolutionary impact on farming in South Carolina and the production of crops in the Southeast.

In 1902 David R. Coker began the first successful commercial cotton-improvement program in the United States based on scientific plant breeding and his philosophy that "The real value of a pound of cotton is the sum of its spinning qualities." He tirelessly promoted educating the farmer in scientific farming methods and became an agricultural statesman for South Carolina.

The sight of a man and a mule plowing is seen less and less in South Carolina.

A tractor can plant, chop weeds, fertilize, and apply chemicals better than any mule.

Cotton from the picker is unloaded into a wagon to be hauled to the gin. This is probably as close as human hands come to the cotton in the field today.

The cotton picker is no longer a bent figure with a heavy sack on his back; he is now, in truth, a veritable machine sucking up the cotton from the field faster than a thousand hands could ever pick it. This model was invented by I. Harvester!

A rare glimpse into the future of South Carolina farms here at the Coker Farm in Hartsville. This picture taken in 1975 shows a new type of wheat ideally suited to areas similar to South Carolina.

Robert Coker holds in his hand the wheat he believes will grow in the golden fields of the future in South Carolina.

The Experimental Farms of Coker became a center for agricultural production and education. Farmers from throughout the South and many parts of the world come here to observe the latest developments and successes in seed-breeding techniques, performances and characteristics of new varieties as well as the most advanced farm practices. They come from near and far—Central and South America, the Near and Middle East, Europe, Asia, Africa, and the Philippines to share knowledge gleaned in the laboratories, greenhouses, nurseries, test plots, and processing plants.

Today Coker experiments go on in locations in ten southern states and in Missouri, California, and New Mexico. Coker developments in seed are used nationwide and abroad. Whether it is cotton, soybeans, corn, small grains, or tobacco, tall, dynamic Robert R. Coker guides the continuing research of this seed empire begun by his father.

The Coker Experimental Farms have attracted national recognition and in 1965 were selected as a Historic Landmark for having made a "highly significant contribution to American agriculture."

HE REPLACED A COMPUTER
WITH PEOPLE

When the phone rings in John W. Park's office it might be Jackie Onassis, Arthur Godfrey, or Mrs. Oscar Hammerstein calling about an order. John Park is president of the largest seed company in the world and scores of celebrities as well as thousands of other flower lovers receive copies of his beautiful catalogue which goes to almost two million gardeners each year.

Park is probably one of the few company executives who recently replaced a computer with people. In tallying orders for special catalogues he found that people make fewer mistakes!

The Park Seed Company is really a giant complex of greenhouses for plant breeding, storage rooms for seeds and bulbs, a highly organized order and shipping department, a garden gift shop—everything that goes with being the world's largest mail-order seed company.

And, if you're near Greenwood, drop in, for "visitors are always welcome," says Park.

John W. Park, the man who replaced a computer with people, president of Park Seed Company at Greenwood.

THE MARGARET MITCHELL
OF HARTSVILLE

"The reason I write about South Carolina is that I adore South Carolina. Her history and her trees and frogs and flowers and people. It wouldn't be possible for me to live anywhere else; nor to set my stories anywhere else. As a matter of fact, is there anywhere else?!"

Her home is set far back from the road and a tree-lined, circular drive curves in front of the tall, white-columned Georgian-style house. It is the perfect setting for novelist Elizabeth Boatwright Coker of Hartsville. Mrs. Coker is a lovely, animated lady and the fact that she appears the prototype of southern womanhood in no way detracts from her charm. Meeting her is like meeting one's favorite heroine from the pages of a historical novel.

She is the widow of one of the South Carolina upcountry's most prominent men, James Lide Coker. The Coker name has long been associated with Hartsville and Hartsville with the Cokers. It would be normal to wonder if there were not more myth than substance to the achievements of such a family, but this is hardly the case. The Cokers continue to make an important contribution to the area in research, industry, and education.

Elizabeth Coker is an unusual and compassionate person. In one of Edward R. Murrow's "This I Believe" programs, she talked to the many boys who had been hit in the face by exploding shells during the Anzio landing. She told of having her face shattered at the age of fifteen and spending two years looking like a gargoyle when she had always been touted as "a beautiful child."

"My front teeth were knocked out, right jawbone broken, cheek crushed in. I hid myself in a back room of the house. I would neither go to school nor see friends.

"Finally, my beloved, beautiful father could stand it no longer and he forced me out into his Overland touring car, top down, to drive slowly around the town waving at people, weeping all the while. But the next day I found the courage to return to High School and to my amazement discovered I'd been elected sponsor of the High School football team during my reclusion! I'll never forget that first game, standing with the team, holding a bouquet of chrysanthemums, grinning toothlessly like crazy and knowing the world was turning properly.

*Elizabeth Boatwright
Coker.*

*On the campus of Coker
College at Hartsville, in
the late afternoon sun, two
children invade the campus
with their thoughts and
games.*

"That has colored my whole life, making me realize it is necessary to go more than the usual mile if one wants to keep in step with one's destiny. It's also given me an empathy with other people's pain and joy.

"I have always been a writer," says Mrs. Coker, who as a college student wrote poetry and short stories that were published in major magazines. "In 1929 after graduating from Converse, I went to New York and worked in the pulps there before I married.

"How did I happen to write my first novel? There was a young colored boy who worked for me before he went into World War II. He was very light-skinned and looked Hawaiian. He was made a sergeant. He wrote me letters telling me he had been accepted as white by the girls in England and he asked me what he was going to do when he came home to Hartsville and had to live on Sixth Street. How was he going to adjust? I thought that was heartbreaking and I wrote a short story about a girl who thought she was white and then when she became an adolescent discovered she was black. At the Columbia University workshop, Glenn Mullen there suggested I turn it into a novel and it became my first, *Daughter of Strangers*."

Elizabeth Coker wrote her first novel at forty. She is now seventy-five and working on her eighth. She recalls with amusement some of her trips to the New York publishing world, in connection with her books.

"They sometimes seem to think we have just come out of the peapatch down here and are very provincial. I don't know whether it's because we don't put on any airs and sit and talk about what we do or where we've been. We talk about little things but we think big things. I've never been able to decide whether it's that or whether they're a little jealous of the South.

"The worst thing happened to me when I was first published. I loved to dress up and wear big hats and look my prettiest. [With the early damage to her face repaired by surgery, Elizabeth Coker was a strikingly beautiful woman.] I would come downstairs at the St. Regis where Jim and I stayed and when the New York interviewers would meet me all dressed up and staying in this lovely hotel, they just immediately bristled. If I had stayed at some fleabag and come down looking sloppy and ugly, everything would have been fine. But they just couldn't believe I had even read a book, much less written one! This prejudice is something we always have to put up with. We've been brought up to look our best. I remember an old nurse of mine saying, 'Put your best foot forward, always.'

"Have women been oppressed in South Carolina? Heavens, I don't think so. Anything that I ever wanted and went after and worked for has always opened up. When I was in college I was one of the great young liberals. We were for opportunity to do anything we wanted to do and that's equal rights opportunity—ERO—which I think is so much smarter than ERA. We were for equal rights for blacks in the twenties.

"Jobs were easy to get then if you were willing to work. We didn't have to fight for the things women do now. If we wanted to work we could. Most women didn't want to. I was for the rights of the individual as opposed to the present day rights of *groups.* The brotherhood of man, I sang. Totally idealistic, romantic, and a dreamer then and now.

"I had some social message themes in my books such as in *Daughter of Strangers. Day of the Peacock* was about the rights of those in the mills to organize and the right not to organize if they didn't want to. The rest of them, I would say, have just been good stories. I'm a storyteller rather than a flag waver. But I have always stood for the dignity of the individual, and that has been my theme.

"The most interesting change in our state to me has been the racial syndrome, because I have always been—as was my husband before his death—very much interested in equality of opportunity for the races. He was one of the first businessmen in the South to have a black foreman in the mill.

"When the cafeteria was opened to blacks, my son was the first to come in and sit down at a table with a black man. He has also been a trustee at Voorhees College. I think one of the greatest changes has been our acceptance of the blacks as coworkers and our willingness to work side by side.

"I have done some substitute teaching in the high school here just because I like to, and I have enjoyed watching the way the two races get along together. You read about the explosive situation in some places but the attitude of the teen-agers toward each other here, from what I have seen, has been good. Most people give Governor Byrnes the credit because he had softened people's attitude even before the Supreme Court decision.

"Late in life, I am discovering that I love to teach. I taught creative writing at Appalachian and discovered I enjoy relating to students, but at the same time I can't give up my writing. I think it's interesting that my first novel was published when I was forty and my first teaching assignment came when I was sixty-four. Wouldn't it be terrible if someone had told me I had to retire at sixty-five? I wouldn't be able to do *The Devil's Horseman,* the book I'm working on now, that I'm sure will be the best one I've ever done.

"What was the title of my last book? My dear, never say the last book—say the latest!"

HE FLIES THE CONFEDERATE FLAG

On the wall of the office hangs a full-length portrait of General Robert E. Lee. In front of it, sitting at a desk, is a silver-haired, distinguished-looking man resembling a Confederate general who has shaved his beard, taken off his uniform, and donned the suit of a Wall Street executive.

Lean, energetic Jack Benfield is a partner and manager of Sullivan-Carson Mill in York. The small town of York's economy is dependent upon the textile industry. Cannon, Huntley, and Talon also have mills here.

In addition to his position as manager of Sullivan-Carson, Jack Benfield is a town commissioner. "Mr. Benfield is probably the smartest man I know and everyone around here respects him," says Mayor Julian Dickerson.

But this is not the entire reason why Benfield is so highly regarded in the community. He is a hero of World War II and South Carolinians respect and admire men who have distinguished themselves on the field of battle. To them, he is Captain Jack Benfield of Merrill's Marauders in the Burma area and the mementos of those days decorate his office. Even a small captured Japanese artillery piece sits on the floor at the left of his desk.

His habit of flying the Confederate flag over the mill has attracted occasional attention from the press as well as from one of the black workers in his mill.

"I explained it to him, though," says Benfield, "and I think he understood. There is nothing about race involved in my flying that flag. To me it represents certain principles. In those days people believed in what they said. They were true to their word. Each morning I see that flag and it's a reminder to Jack Benfield to keep it straight today." Benfield is concerned about a loss of moral values in present-day American business and society. To him the Confederate flag symbolizes high principles and honorable conduct.

Sullivan-Carson Mill makes elastic, clothing tape, zipper tape, label tape, and webbing. There are one hundred and sixty employees and Benfield goes out of his way to keep in personal touch with them, even going on the "graveyard shift" once a month to speak to people he would never see during his daytime office hours.

There are many modern new mills throughout South Carolina and times have changed for textile employees. Benfield believes there is far more opportunity now for the children of millworkers and the workers themselves, if they want to try other fields, than there was thirty years ago. The old

J. T. Benfield of York works in his office under a portrait of Robert E. Lee. A Japanese machine gun, part of the decor, was captured when he was with Merrill's Marauders in Burma in World War II.

company-owned mill village is becoming a thing of the past. Most mill-workers own their own homes which are often scattered throughout the town so that the example of a neighbor's career has an influence on children who once grew up knowing no other way of life.

Benfield is genuinely concerned that employees with an interest in continuing their education go on to night school in York for training and has told several people who were considering other jobs, "If you can find a better position, I will do everything possible to help you."

How does he feel about promoting women? "I would like to see more women at higher-level positions in the mill. We have tried it a couple of times here, but the loom-fixer level is usually impassable. There are huge gears that have to be lifted and, so far, it just hasn't worked."

Most South Carolina mills are still not unionized. "I consider their tactics crude and threatening," says Benfield whose employees have not voted the union in.

Born and raised in York County, Benfield graduated from Clemson College and went on to Philadelphia to work with his present firm. He was always hopeful, if not actively scheming, to get back to South Carolina. He knew that his boss was interested in building another mill and so one day he took a copy of a Southern Railway ad that said, "Look Ahead—Look South" and left it on his superior's desk.

The ad had its hoped-for effect and with Benfield in charge of scouting for a site, going South is just what Sullivan-Carson did. The place he selected for their new plant was his hometown of York and the decision has proved beneficial both for the company and the town.

MISS BESSIE'S MOST VIVID DAY

The day which is most vivid in her mind is July 14, 1918. Lemon-yellow day lilies were in bloom, white clouds drifted above the Winnsboro town clock. Bessie Hood was the sheriff's wife. She was in her garden that morning while her husband was waiting for his two deputies to bring a black man from Columbia to stand trial.

By nine o'clock small knots of people had begun to gather in groups of two or three down at the railroad station and more were standing outside the courthouse on Main Street. Sheriff Hood had stationed a deputy in the crowd, and he paced back and forth himself, waiting. The train pulled into

*The classic lines of the
Fairfield County
Courthouse were designed
by South Carolina's own
architect, Robert Mills,
who studied architecture
with Thomas Jefferson.*

The curved metal stairs to the upper floor of the courthouse remind one of the graceful stairs of the public buildings of Europe.

the depot. His two deputies and the prisoner got off, the sheriff joined them and the four men started across the street toward the courthouse.

The prisoner was charged with the rape of a Winnsboro housewife, feeling was running high and Hood was apprehensive. The thought of a lynching attempt had occurred to him but he knew his fellow townsmen well and they knew him. He doubted they would try to take the prisoner, but any number of ugly things were a possibility. Suppose something happened among the crowd to frighten the prisoner and he tried to jerk away. How would the crowd react? Suppose two or three of the town's less reputable characters who had already had a few drinks tried to start something?

Hood and his deputies walked one on each side and another behind him. Now, they had crossed the road and were in front of the courthouse. The crowd watched intently but quietly. Hood's plan was to take the prisoner up the flight of stairs on the north side of the courthouse and into the entrance to the courtroom on the second floor. This seemed the quickest and most direct route.

Thus far, there had been no angry shouts or actions from the crowd. Everything was going well, but he would feel better when they were inside the building. He was determined to prevent trouble and see that the man was brought to trial.

They reached the bottom of the steps that led up the side of the building to the courtroom. He and his men huddled more closely than ever around the prisoner shielding him with their own bodies. They were halfway up the stairs now. Suddenly, came the loud blast of a shotgun. Wheeling around even as some of the shot entered his body, Hood saw a smoking shotgun pointed upward being reloaded. He drew his pistol and fired back. The man fell dead.

The sheriff turned back to the prisoner who, along with one of the deputies, had been shot. Supporting the wounded prisoner, the lawmen hurried up the stairs and managed to reach the courtroom. Hood carried the defendant over to the dock. Then he walked to the judge's stand and sank to the floor. A crowd quickly gathered around the wounded men and someone went out to get the local doctor only to find that he was out of town.

A deputy was sent to fetch the sheriff's wife, Bessie Hood. He found her arranging flowers in her kitchen. All he told her was, "Mr. Hood wants to see you."

"I didn't know what had happened until I got up to the courtroom. Mr. Hood and a black man were lying on the floor. A deputy was lying on a table. I stepped over the black man to get to my husband. Blood was coming from my husband's coat sleeve. A man in the courtroom who said he was a doctor from Columbia was trying to help. He said he couldn't get to the bleeding and I said, why don't you cut that sleeve off. He did and discovered that the main artery in my husband's arm was pierced. Later we found he had twenty-three perforations.

Mrs. Bessie Richardson of Winnsboro holds the American flag she crocheted. Her first husband was Sheriff Hood who died protecting a black prisoner.

"There were no cars then to take him to the hospital at Columbia so they phoned the Southern Railroad to send a coach from Columbia to pick up the wounded. All my husband said was, 'Bessie, go home first and change your dress.' I was still in my cotton house dress.

"The train left Winnsboro about noon and I went with him. I thought we would never reach Columbia. My husband lay flat on the floor in the baggage coach with the deputy lying near him. The black man had died shortly after I reached the courtroom.

"While we were sitting beside my husband on the floor of the baggage car, my father said, 'Adam, who shot you?' I tried to hold his head in my arms so he could answer, but he was too weak. When the train reached the crossing in Columbia, men were waiting there with stretchers to carry them to the hospital. My husband was operated on that afternoon and they brought him back to his room. He turned his head and his lips moved as he tried to speak to me, but he couldn't.

"I remember the sun was setting and a glow came in through the window and was on him. He died a few minutes after six."

If you should see a white-haired lady in her mid-eighties gardening, driving her car downtown to shop or chatting with a friend in the post office, it could be Miss Bessie, once a pretty blond girl with blue eyes whose husband died defending his black prisoner.

A VIETNAM VETERAN RETURNS
TO WINNSBORO

◆

When Webster Anderson was in high school he knew what he wanted to be. He wanted to be a soldier and for a long time it was a good way of life for a young man who had dropped out of school. Now, he was eager to make up for that and he gradually worked his way up to being a sergeant.

Then came Vietnam and on October 15, 1967, Sergeant Anderson and his unit were near Tam Ky when the Vietcong launched a fierce suicide attack. Grenades shattered at his feet and blew off both of Anderson's legs. Painfully mutilated, he managed to crawl back to a foxhole and fell into it with another severely wounded comrade.

A short distance away an enemy soldier saw the two men in their foxhole and hurled a grenade squarely at them, sure he would finish them off. Anderson groped desperately in the mud for the grenade, but before he could pitch it back it exploded in his right hand blowing it off. Refusing medical aid, he continued to direct the fire of his gun crew at the enemy.

During the time he was in the hospital he was in good spirits cheering up other wounded veterans. While he recuperated, he lay for long hours thinking about where he would live and what he would do with his future. It would not be Philadelphia where he had been stationed, he decided. It was hard enough for a person without a handicap to survive in a big city. He decided that he would go back to South Carolina and Winnsboro, the town where he had grown up.

"When Winnsboro turned out to celebrate 'Webster Anderson Day' it really showed me how much people here thought of me," says Anderson, who was awarded the Congressional Medal of Honor.

"I thought about this decision a lot, for I didn't know whether it would work or what it would be like to come home after so long. But the people here have been really great to me. Somehow, in a small place they seem to care more about each other."

Winnsboro did more than just have a special day honoring their returning hero. Anderson has a wife and three children, so the townspeople got together and built them an attractive, four-bedroom colonial-style home.

When he first returned as a triple amputee, Anderson was not sure what he would find to do, but his hobby of fixing TV sets and radios soon grew into a business. He has his own little building for his repair work just a few steps from his home.

"Everyone has periods of feeling discouraged, and I've had mine," says Anderson. "While I was in the hospital I talked to a lot of men that were pretty far down. I try to be a Christian and some of the time I think I got through to them and gave them hope. I was raised in the church like most people around here, and I think all of us have got to give something to God.

"I've never regretted coming back."

Webster Anderson and his wife in front of his home built for them by the people of Winnsboro.

THE MAN WHO BROUGHT
NORTHERN INDUSTRY SOUTH

◆

In the tall, white, starkly impressive building on the Greenville skyline on the fifth floor are the elegant offices of Daniel, one of the world's largest construction companies. Employees walk noiselessly across thick carpets, secretaries sit at desks as large as most executives', walls are covered with dark, rich paneling, and the furniture resembles that of a grand southern mansion.

The master of this "mansion" is a Pennsylvania Yankee with a deceptively soft voice and iron determination. Within reach of his desk is an illuminated world globe, for he manages a company that operates not only in the United States but in Canada, South America, the Dominican Republic, and Free Europe. After co-ordinating activities from the New York office of Daniel for ten years, Charles Cox now lives and works in Greenville as corporate president and chief operating officer of the company.

A man who has lived most of his life in the North, Cox says "I believe to be truly part of a southern community you have to adapt. I found it natural. People here in the South are very gracious. There is a lot of difference in the attitude toward life and the warm personal relationships."

Cox is one of many Northerners who are "adapting" and forming a substantial part of the leadership of the rapidly industrializing state. At first as New York manager of sales for Daniel, later as general manager of construction in the United States, and recently as president, Charles Cox has brought many industries to South Carolina. He is quick to share the credit, saying, "Everyone in our organization has taken a personal pride in assisting companies that are unhappy either for political reasons or due to labor rates to relocate where they can have a happier life and make more money.

"South Carolina has come a long way in the past twenty years from the early days of a predominantly textile economy. This change has been an exciting process. Ten years ago maybe nine out of ten plants we were building were in some way related to the textile industry. Now, maybe one out of ten is related. There is tremendous diversification—aluminum reduction, all metalworking facilities, the chemical and petroleum industries, plants serving the utilities, oil, pulp and paper industries, heavy equipment, building materials, automotive products, plastics.

"People sometimes think that when companies decide to come South

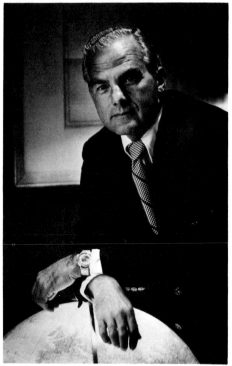

*The Daniel International
Corporation is the nation's second
largest publicly owned general-
contracting firm. In 1975 they had
a backlog of eight billion dollars
in construction contracts.*

*"I can build it for you faster,
better, and at less cost," is the
motto of Charles W. Cox,
president of Daniel International
Corporation.*

they decide one day and a few months later move into their new plant in the southeast. It just doesn't work that way. There may not be the sales volume here. So, the easiest thing was to have Daniel build warehouses.

"A company would send bearings down to their warehouse in South Carolina and the warehouse would distribute them. As the market grew they found they were selling enough ball bearings to build a manufacturing plant here. This became true with hundreds of industries. You don't make the investment in a plant when you know your sales and marketing in the South are still immature. The logical thing is to put an inexpensive warehouse here, develop a marketing capability, and as the South grows industrially you build your manufacturing facility. Ten years ago this is exactly what happened.

"In the second generation, the warehouses no longer satisfied the appetite because the market has grown to such an extent they can afford to build manufacturing plants.

"But now we are facing a problem. We have grown at such a fast pace that the South is getting more than its share of the gross national product and in the process of growth, we have basically absorbed the people. The South's future growth will be impaired unless we find a way to upgrade minority labor. We are utilizing 95 per cent of our white labor but possibly only 10 to 20 per cent of our black labor and Daniel is doing everything we can to change this. We have our own in-company training programs and we are also working very closely on curriculum with the technical schools.

"We must do everything possible to provide our black minority group with technical skills if South Carolina and the South is to continue its industrial growth spurt of the past decade."

A modern-day John Henry works on building foundation.

FOOD FROM THE SEA

Picture an elaborate restaurant in New York City. The menu contains the most exotic food from all over the world. A customer devours his scampi with obvious relish. "Where do these delectable shrimp come from?" he asks the waiter, who replies, "Sir, there is only one place in the world, Charleston, South Carolina. They are called Carolaysian shrimp."

Actually, these shrimp are not on the market yet. If and when they are it will be due to the imagination and efforts of Dr. Victor G. Burrell, director of the South Carolina Marine Resources Research Institute near Charleston.

One of his many projects here involves the Malaysian prawn, a variety of shrimp with excellent possibilities for cultivating in fresh waters.

"This is a shrimp that we hope we can grow on a 'put and take' basis in coastal fresh waters," says Dr. Burrell. They require salt water for only one brief stage of their development. They can even be raised in artificial salt water, so they can probably be grown in any part of the state. This species is native to Hawaii and Malaysia. We use them because they grow rapidly, will breed and spawn in captivity, and have many attributes our native species don't have."

How well do these shrimp feed in the temperature of our waters?

"They feed poorly for about half the year but we are trying to improve the growing period by genetics and crossbreeding. During the period they feed well, they grow very rapidly. Even with the short growing season we were able to produce about fourteen hundred pounds to the acre which looks very hopeful. They mature to about a sixteenth of a pound which is a nice size shrimp."

Shrimp is not the only form of marine life Dr. Burrell believes has possibilities.

"We are working on the culture of both oysters and soft-shell crabs. These things are being handled differently here than would occur in nature and that is when you start calling it 'culture.' We hope the people in the present crab pot fishery, once we work out the techniques, will start taking the peeler crabs out of the regular catch and putting them into floats to shed, because the peeler crabs have about ten times the value of the hard crab. I think this can be a very profitable venture for our fisheries."

Why has South Carolina not developed the soft-shell-crab industry?

"People down here are not as sophisticated as people in the fishing indus-

try in Virginia. They don't really know how to tell a peeler crab—a crab ready to shed.

"Our industry is actually behind the Chesapeake in more ways than one. They have just recently begun to use the crab pot compared to Virginia where it began in 1939. It came here in the late 1950s.

"We also have good oyster potential in the South Carolina estuaries. But the oyster industry has to have cultivation, for oysters are not a resource you can leave alone and then harvest as a quality product. A crop must be produced regularly and in order to do this you must increase its value. We think we will be able to do this, but at present our oysters grow between the tides, that is, they are exposed between tides. These oysters are misshapen, hard to harvest, and hard to shuck. They command a very low price.

"We believe we can re-establish subtidal oyster culture in South Carolina by using some of the methods developed in the Chesapeake Bay area. Oysters grow very fast in our waters and I think it will be just a matter of time until we have subtidal oyster culture."

Under the watchful eye of Dr. Burrell, the new seafoods of the future are hatching beneath the waters of the South Carolina coast.

Dr. John Mark Dean at the University of South Carolina is an outspoken advocate of some major additions to aquaculture research.

"The emphasis now is on the cultivation and production of luxury food products rather than essential food products," says Dr. Dean.

"Work is not going on at present on those systems that we know historically would be cheap to produce and therefore meet the world protein need. Instead it is lobster, shrimp, oysters; and the fish that is being cultivated is catfish, pompano, and trout. There is extensive work on trout. We are talking about fish that have to be sold for well over a dollar a pound and most people can't afford that. You have to feed them 40 per cent protein and this is a high-protein diet. If you take that 40 per cent and feed it to a fish you are actually wasting energy.

"This protein must be converted and there is a loss in the conversion.

What we should be doing is trying to find a herbivore, that is something that eats grass in the ocean and converts grass to protein. But, we're not working on those species. That is my quarrel with aquaculture generally.

"For example, the fish that has broad implications for aquaculture and that is being worked on in Hawaii and Israel is the mullet. We need to work on fish that eat plankton or detritus. Mullet is one of them. It has worldwide distribution. The Japanese will buy all we can produce. It's a fish with great commercial potential.

"But when proposals are submitted to study the reproductive biology of mullet, they aren't funded. They go to Sea Grant and are turned down. They want you to work on lobsters or shrimp. They have developed their priorities and I'm in the minority on what I think we should be studying.

"Oysters are a tremendous aquaculture beast. What we really need now is someone with the capital to risk growing oysters. I think they have the greatest potential of any species.

"Oysters aren't necessarily the food of the few because one of the things oysters can do is harvest the things that are floating in the water. They are filter feeders. If you dump treated sewage from a plant into the water it grows algae. I don't make a value judgment on sewage. It is simply a nutrient out of place. The French and Spanish grow tremendous quantities of mussels in the bays they dump the sewage into. Then they move them into clean water and let them go through a cleansing process which they simply do by pumping water. They take up the nutrients which have been packaged by the plankton and then they filter out the plankton. That's feasible and people are working with this.

"If the sewage effluent was put in ponds and lagoon systems and the algae allowed to grow, we could pump the sewage from the waterfront communities back into the pine trees. There, ponds the size of a large room would make this system work. Oysters can't grow in there because it's fresh water, but there is a clam that's a *pest* right now called corvicula. It grows about two inches or so and it's in our fresh-water systems.

"It's not a commercial clam as such, but what we're talking about is simply converting waste nutrients into protein. Once that protein is packaged by the clams, then grind it up and you will have plenty of protein to feed chickens, make fertilizer out of, or put in cat food. You may do the same thing with fish. You may actually use a fish that you and I will not eat to package protein, menhaden for example. We don't eat menhaden but they graze at the primary level. They feed on plankton and then we harvest them.

"The dimension of the problem is where I differ from the traditional aquaculture people. They want to convert protein into an immediately marketable product—trout, salmon, pompano. This requires too great an energy subsidy. Our natural eco systems such as the salt-water tidelands are very efficient in terms of utilizing energy."

SOUTH CAROLINA BECKONS THE GIRL
FROM OHIO

◆

"I don't know whether you ever saw Anita Bryant in her orange juice commercial sing, 'In Carolina in the Morning'? That commercial was very popular and I used to hear it at night on TV in Ohio and I thought I'd die if I didn't come to Beaufort!" says Cheryl Cotterman.

Cheryl and her husband, Ed, were born and raised in Ohio. Her brother was in the Marine Corps at Parris Island and each winter on their way to Florida they stopped to see him.

"We started coming through Beaufort. We liked the area and fell in love with the people. While we were here we talked with the chamber of commerce and people in the town and asked them what it needed. Everyone said that Beaufort needed a good restaurant so we decided to come here and open one. We had had no training in the restaurant business. My husband traveled and sold radio time and I owned a beauty salon in Ohio.

"We looked at several homes and I wanted to buy the first one I saw because I wanted to move to Beaufort so badly. But, my husband said, 'No, the location isn't good.' Our real estate lady said, 'The Anchorage is for sale, a big old house on Bay Street, and I just want you to look at it. It was built before the Revolution and it is right on the waterfront.'

"That afternoon we came in and the poor house had been closed up for five years. Although there had been considerable renovation the house just had a sad look about it. My husband said, 'Well, we're not interested,' so we went back to Ohio.

"Two days later our realtor called us and said, 'What do you kids think of the Anchorage?' Ed said, 'Honey, what shall we tell her?' I looked at him as though I were affluent as hell and I said, 'Why not? We'll buy the Anchorage. I want to go to South Carolina' and he said all right.

"About two weeks later we came down, signed the papers, and then we proceeded to sell our property in Ohio. We sold everything we had other than a few pieces of furniture and personal things. We packed it up in a U-Haul Truck and I drove our Oldsmobile. I really felt like a pioneer.

"That was in February and it took us until July to open up. We completely renovated the house. Then we had to find a chef. We asked around and everyone including the chamber of commerce made suggestions. Our attorney, Mr. Harker—poor Michael!—we could never have opened up if it hadn't been for him. Being from Ohio, I knew nothing about the South Carolina laws and being a damn Yankee, I get excited much quicker than the people in Beaufort do. And so every day, twice a day, I'd call him and say, 'Michael, they won't let us do this, they won't let us do that,' and Michael would say, 'Calm down, we'll take care of it.'

"We opened up during the Water Festival and you know, when you have a new place everybody comes. The first day we had about a hundred and fifty people standing in line. The second day we had a commitment for a huge wedding reception and the third day the cook asked for a raise. By this time we had exhausted most of our funds and borrowed everything we could from the bank. So, I told my husband, 'Honey, we just can't give him a raise'—so he left.

"My husband asked, 'What the hell are we going to do now?' And I said, 'I will cook.' He said, 'You'll do what?'"

Cheryl Cotterman had never cooked for anything larger than a family group in her life.

Cheryl Cotterman.

"I said, it's either do it or the whole damn thing goes down the drain. So, I cooked for over three months. Now, I'm happy to say I have a good woman who used to cook at the Gold Eagle and we have a couple who do the cooking at night, and I think we're finally getting the team together.

"It's been a struggle, but I've loved every minute of it because I like people. But this is my home and when the people don't come it's as though I had invited them to a dinner party and they didn't show up.

"I'm very nervous and these people are so quiet and easygoing. To me it's very relaxing. They are extremely kind and helpful. We didn't know anyone here outside of my brother. Whenever we have needed anything, personal or financial, everyone has been very good to us. The people at the Bank of Beaufort, at the water department, the light department, all of them have been very friendly. I have never met more sincere people in my life.

"The funniest thing that happened to me was when we first opened up. On a Saturday night we had a buffet because, thank God, I was smart enough to realize I couldn't turn out orders because that takes experience and knowledge. This one night we served probably two hundred and fifty people and I came upstairs dragging, and I mean dragging. Because I was exhausted from remodeling the house, opening, and the pressures. I came upstairs where there was a little chair outside the lounge and my husband said, 'Honey, what would you like?' and I said give me a scotch. And I sat down there with my scotch in my hand and some lady came in and said, 'Humph, they even allow their kitchen help upstairs!' and looked right at me. I just looked at her and smiled and went on drinking my drink."

THE SMALL TOWN

Since South Carolina is obviously a state of small towns, what does this mean in terms of the American experience?

To be President of America in the nineteenth century, to be born in a log cabin was a very distinct asset. In the twentieth century the road to the White House led from the small town.

Ike, born in Denison, Texas, grew up in Abilene, Kansas, the quintessence of the American small town. His father was a mechanic.

Harry Truman was born in Lamar, Missouri, a small town, his father a farmer. He grew up in another small town named Independence, Missouri.

Herbert Hoover was born in West Branch, Iowa.

The railroad station at North, South Carolina.

The paving bricks in the square at Abbeville were brought over from England.

Far from city streets, the fishing village of McClellanville typifies the peace and quiet of the small towns.

Across the state there are clocks. This is the clock tower on the campus at Clemson University.

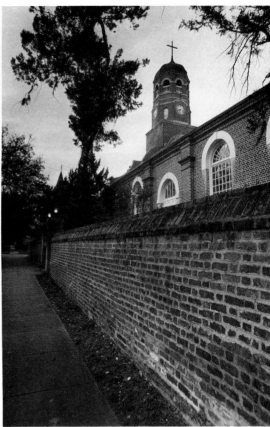

Prince George Winyah Episcopal Church at Georgetown was founded in 1781 and named after King George II. It was occupied by British troops during the Revolution.

Opposite: *The British were convinced that every Presbyterian church was a center for rebellion and every Presbyterian preacher an agent of sedition. This is the McClellanville Presbyterian Church, as it is today, surrounded by the beauty of live oaks and azaleas.*

Barnwell Rhett, the fire-eating "Father of Secession," is said to have drawn up a draft of the Ordinance of Secession in the East Room of this house, later called "Secession House."

Calvin Coolidge came from Plymouth Notch, Vermont, the son of a small town storekeeper and farmer.

Harding came from Blooming Grove (now Corsica), Ohio, the son of a farmer.

Woodrow Wilson was the son of a Presbyterian minister and was born in Staunton, Virginia.

The list goes on and on. If the small towns of America have given this country nothing else, they have given us our Presidents.

Since South Carolinian Henry Laurens affixed his signature to the Constitution of the United States two centuries ago, less than half a dozen men in two centuries who reached the pinnacle of the power and the glory of the White House did it without having walked with the common townsman.

To be from a small town means the insights gained in the long summers of going barefoot to school when spring comes, of passing the time of day with the village eccentric, of watching the character of one's neighbors unfold in daily life, and of cultivating the human relationships necessary to become a big frog in a small puddle first.

After the Civil War the North had, with invisible ink, written a new amendment into the Constitution that was to last almost a century—no man born in the South could live in the White House.

And so, the small town boys from southern states became members of the cabinet—the Baruchs, the Byrnes, the Daniels. But this will change, and, along with it, the small town experience may again be valued.

St. John's Lutheran Church at Walhalla looms above this mountain town looking as if it might have belonged on the Midwest prairie. Many German immigrants came north from the port city of Charleston and settled here.

HILTON HEAD ISLAND

Hilton Head Island is the best of all possible worlds in which nothing jarring or discordant ever enters. It has been called a veritable paradise of the South Carolina low country where the climate is always mild and the setting one of magnificent natural beauty. Harbour Town is part of the magnificent development of Sea Pines, a bit of the Mediterranean brought to South Carolina. It is particularly beautiful at dusk when the lights of the buildings are reflected across the water.

Although it is one of America's newest resorts, the island is one of the nation's oldest in terms of history and prehistory. The first men, Indian hunters wandering down the coast, probably arrived here ten thousand years ago. Great Indian ceremonial shell rings found on the island indicate that Indians had permanently settled here eight hundred years before work began on the great pyramids of Egypt. The modern history of the island began when Fred C. Hack, on a timber-buying trip, visited the island by boat. He and Joseph B. Fraser, Sr., a retired general, were so impressed with its beauty that they bought the island and launched America's most unique island resort. The view on the preceding pages is the harbor at Sea Pines Plantation.

The Fraser family pioneered in developing what has been praised as America's outstanding seaside development totally compatible with nature.

Fred Hack stands by the bridge which he helped obtain for the island. He was buying timber when he first discovered Hilton Head. It was incredibly beautiful, he says. He felt almost as if he were an explorer who stepped out of the seventeenth century and for the first time really saw the island. It was remote then, reached only by a slow boat from the mainland. "I built the bridge and the Frasers came across it," says Hack. Mr. Hack has also played an important part in the development of Hilton Head.

WHERE THE REVOLUTION
IN THE SOUTH BEGAN

Concord Bridge was where the Revolution began in the North, but how many have ever heard of Ninety Six? The first blood shed in the Revolutionary War occurred in the South at Ninety Six in November 1775. The town was so named because traders calculated it was ninety-six miles from an Indian town named Keowee.

Protected by a makeshift stockade of fence rails, bales of straw, and ani-

Archeologists are gradually unearthing the entrenchments surrounding the Star Fort at Ninety Six.

An enthusiastic busload of school children arrives to tour the Revolutionary War battlefield at Ninety Six.

Re-enactment of the Battle of Camden. The original battle was an American defeat.

mal hides, five hundred and sixty-two Patriots blazed away at an attacking force of Tories three times their number. Hostilities began in South Carolina with considerably more flair than the brief encounter at Concord.

Eleven o'clock on Sunday morning, November 19, a force of almost two thousand Tories arrived at the courthouse in Ninety Six with drums beating and colors flying, and demanded the surrender of the Patriots. But the Patriots refused and, despite being outnumbered three to one, they opened fire. The shooting continued into the night. It began again Monday and lasted until sunset Tuesday when the Tories under a white flag, flown from the jail in which they had taken cover, sent a message asking for a conference.

There had been frost the night before and the smoke from the breakfast fires hung lazy and blue in the crisp air as this young wife washed her pots and pans. It was a scene from the past not painted in oils but alive, just as it really was in South Carolina when many of the young wives went along with their husbands, for in much of the upcountry the only safety was with the troops, no matter which side.

The men had marched off to take part in the celebration of the first southern land battle of the Revolution, leaving the wives to clean the camp. And this, probably, was the way it was two hundred years ago not only at Ninety Six, but at Eutaw Springs, Cowpens, and dozens of other small skirmish sites and camps scattered across the state.

Two hundred years later the
sound of American drums and
British muskets echo across the
rolling land where the first clash
of arms took place in the South.
In November of 1775, Patriots and
Loyalists fought here at Ninety
Six, now a national historic site.
This was the southern Concord
Bridge, the first land battle of
the Revolution in the South.

Tents and trees, utensils and uniforms are authentic and perhaps even the faces.
Could this be Colonel Ferguson beside his tent on the morning before the mountain men attack?

An army of British provincial troops and Loyalist militia under Major Patrick Ferguson was encamped on the summit of Kings Mountain on October 7, 1780. By the end of the day his forces had been attacked and his camp overrun by American frontiersmen. Ferguson died in battle and was buried under this pile of rocks not far from where he fell. He died not knowing that he had been promoted to colonel or that the basic idea of a breech-loading rifle which he had designed would be used by armies around the world. For Ferguson it was the end of a promising military career. For the Americans it was a turning point in the Revolution in the South.

The beginning of the Revolution in South Carolina was typical of the character of the people of the state. When they think they are right they dig in and fight. Both sides battled at the town of Ninety Six for three days (without a British officer on the field) which certainly makes Concord seem a mere skirmish.

Later Ninety Six became famous as a key fort in Cornwallis' defense system in the South and the American Army laid siege to it. When the British finally abandoned Ninety Six, they burned the village as they departed. South Carolina is the only state in the Union where villages, towns, and churches have been burned twice by angry enemy armies. It is hard to conceive of the effect this would have had on the history of Ohio or New York.

Ninety Six also had the distinction of being one of the last battles of the Revolution. After the fall of Charleston in May 1780, the British Army garrisoned a chain of outposts stretching in an arc from Georgetown, South Carolina, to Augusta, Georgia. Their principal fortress was Ninety Six.

Using this chain of forts as a base, Cornwallis planned to launch a campaign into Virginia to crush the American revolt. The town of Ninety Six with its stockade and earthen fort in the shape of a star was commanded by a New York Tory named John Cruger. Lieutenant Colonel Cruger had manned the fort with five hundred and fifty well-trained and disciplined Tory troops from New York, New Jersey, and South Carolina. Village, courthouse, and jail were completely enclosed within a stockade. On high ground east of the village was the Star Fort connected to the town by a trench.

After the Battle of Guilford Courthouse in North Carolina where

Nathaniel Greene brought Cornwallis to a standstill, Greene turned his attention to subduing the Star Fort and marched to attack it. By now, Henry Lee, Francis Marion, Thomas Sumter, and Andrew Pickens had driven the British from the smaller outposts at Georgetown, Fort Motte, and Fort Granby.

For twenty-eight days Greene laid siege to Ninety Six. Then news arrived that Lord Rawdon and two thousand men were marching from Charleston to relieve the besieged garrison. With time running out, Greene tried to storm the fort and was repulsed. He reluctantly withdrew before the overwhelming British reinforcements could arrive.

Rawdon soon realized that the post was too isolated to hold and the garrison was later abandoned, with local Tories retreating to Charleston under the protection of the British. The redcoats had lost all of the upcountry and were confined to a small coastal enclave until the following year when the War ended at Yorktown.

His name might have been Belk or Ivey or B. C. Moore, and he is running the first country store. Sutlers like this man at the muster at Ninety Six could always be found near army camps selling their wares of mugs, pipes, tobacco, cooking utensils, or whatever was needed. Camps for both sides were more than military stopovers; they were the only places offering security to those who believed in the same cause. The quill and ledger, the merchandise on display, and the spirit of free enterprise began here and led to the modern shopping center.

BATTLE AT CAMDEN

PICTURE ESSAY
CEMETERY AT BEAUFORT

◆———

In St. Helena's Episcopal cemetery at Beaufort are some unusual markers of some unusual people. Major John La Boularderie de Treville, wounded at the Battle of Savannah, served his adopted country as major of the 4th Regular South Carolina Artillery; the British lieutenant and ensign killed in battle near Gray's Hill in 1779, Captain James Stuart murdered by Indians in Oregon in 1851 "while leading his men brilliantly to victory," a boy who served the Confederacy while a Citadel cadet had C.S.A. engraved on his marker forty-five years later, and a young Confederate captain named Paul Hamilton who died at twenty after serving "gallantly" in thirty battles. Some of the old raised stones became impromptu operating tables during the Civil War.

Here lie the bodies of
LIEUT.
WILLIAM CALDERWOOD
and
ENSIGN JOHN FINLEY
of Col. Prevost's British
troops. Killed in battle near
Gray's Hill Feb. 3, 1779.
Buried here Feb. 5, 1779.

Rest in peace

BREV. CAPT. JAMES STUART,
REG. MOUNTED RIFLES. U.S.A.
WHO "FELL MORTALLY WOUNDED
IN BATTLE WITH THE INDIANS IN
OREGON," WHILE LEADING HIS MEN
"GALLANTLY TO VICTORY."
JUNE 17TH 1851.
GEN. JONES' REPORT
HE WAS A GIFTED. ACCOMPLISH
_____ABLE HEARTED. GENTLEM__

ALBERT RHETT HEYWARD
BORN IN BEAUFORT, S.C.
JAN. 10, 1846
DIED NEAR COLUMBIA, S.C.
NOV. 24, 1910
CORPORAL CITADEL CADETS C.S.A.

THE MAN WHO BOUGHT THE PAST

Fifteen years ago when P. E. Cox realized his dream of purchasing an old country store, he was sure that he had outdistanced the twentieth century. The store in Irmo was almost a hundred years old and he playfully renamed it the Ancient Irmese Country Store.

Irmo, west of Columbia, began in the 1880s as a whistle stop on the Columbia, Newberry and Laurens Railroad. When the small farming community incorporated in 1890, the citizens decided to name it Irmo after the secretary of the railroad, C. J. Iredell, and the president, H. C. Moseley.

The village was the home of many German settlers, including the ancestors of the present mayor, Furman Youngener, who still farms and retains his German accent mingled with a southern drawl.

After graduating from the University of South Carolina Law School, Cox went on to become an FBI man in New York. But he soon tired of the big city and felt that he would be happier back in South Carolina. There was his longtime dream of owning a country store and why couldn't he do that and practice law, too? Furnishing a cubbyhole at the rear with his law-

P. E. Cox checks over a grocery list in his country store.

Can a lawyer and former FBI man find happiness in a country store? P. E. Cox can.

A quick hand darts into the candy jar at the Irmo country store.

books, desk, and diplomas on the wall, he moved in to spend his days answering the calls of clients in his office and selling merchandise to customers in the store.

"What do you need, a chicken?" says Cox as he waits on a lady at the meat counter. His store has a cozy, twilight sort of atmosphere, none of that harsh supermarket glare for Cox who has kept everything as it was—right back in the nineteenth century. He continues to order old-fashioned stock items and has even added some antiques.

But while Cox was happily contemplating the purchase of the store to be run by himself and his family in the good old ways, progress was even then gathering itself for a mighty leap which would encompass Irmo and the surrounding area.

As he opened his doors to his first customers, the plot to bring Irmo into the twentieth century had already begun in the mind of an imaginative real estate developer named Michael J. Mungo. When Mungo looked at Irmo he saw more than a slumbering village—he saw its nearness to Lake Murray, its lack of slums, and, above all, its convenience to the city of Columbia.

It was not long before industry saw the same advantages and General Electric came to Irmo with a huge plant, followed soon afterward by Allied Chemical. Mungo was ready. He began to build the housing developments that were to make him a multimillionaire. Despite the joke of a Columbia radio announcer that "Irmo was a good place to be *from*," Mungo's persuasiveness began to convince literally thousands of people that Columbia was the best place to be from and they began to move into his new housing developments at Irmo.

An island of tranquillity—the Ancient Irmese Country Store.

From the dim recesses of his Ancient Irmese Store, Cox watched while his community of five hundred people became the nucleus of a thriving area of twenty-five thousand residents.

Driving through South Carolina often gives the visitor the feeling of having been suddenly dropped into the pages of a history book. But entering Irmo is just the opposite, for it *is* passing from the present into the future and it's just as odd a sensation. Everything is new—the attractive housing developments, the up-to-date fire station, and the modernistic new school all give the impression that the last bricklayer left just a few minutes ago.

P. E. Cox shakes his head and says, "Only one thing stands still here in Irmo and that's my store." The old country store stands amid all the commotion, untouched, a popular meeting place for both new and ancient Irmese who enjoy stopping to shop and chat with the gregarious proprietor. And it's only an illusion that time stands still within these walls, for Irmo is part of the change that marks much of the state of South Carolina in the seventies.

A PICTURE PORTFOLIO

Two fishermen in an inlet near John's Island.

Sea oats along the South Carolina coast.

A balancing act is done by the surfer at Myrtle Beach as he rides the crest of a wave.

Clemson became a university in 1964 after beginning full-time operation as an agricultural college in 1893. More than two hundred campus buildings have been built since 1950 and training is offered in fifty-five graduate studies and hundreds of occupations and professions.

Ruins of Old Sheldon Parish Church. Sheldon Church has the distinction of being burned twice by invading armies—in 1779 by the British and in 1865 by the federal army. Annual services are held here the second Sunday after Easter.

It looks as if Box 74 on Route 2 is out of business as bulldozers near Greenwood clear a path for a new highway.

Symbol of the vanished tenant farmer; this is an abandoned tenant house on farmland where machines have replaced human hands.

The Hammock Shop on Highway 17 near Pawley's Island is not just a store but a veritable museum of low country history with a dozen buildings set amidst pines and azalea. E. H. Lachicotte loves the area and has created this setting of an old schoolhouse, plantation, tobacco barn, and other typical low country buildings to display South Carolina crafts as well as sell the famous Pawley's Island hammocks.

Opposite: *The Camden Cup Race is one of the highlights of South Carolina horse racing. This picture shot at the stable at Camden ran as a Miscellany page in* Life.

Lydia put her hands behind her head, looked at the ceiling of the dark bedroom and thought about the columns to the old house. Each day going to school and coming home again she walked by them. Now, they would be dark against the sky, the weeds and vines just visible in the moonlight. What did they mean standing there day after day? Once there was a house there. . . . yes, a house and a curved drive with carriages gliding up to the pillars and all of a sudden it wasn't a myth anymore. There had been parties with handsome young men in gray uniforms and the past was real, just as alive as she was. That was what the pillars had been saying to her.

"We fought, but fought in vain, and though our banner may never again be unfurled, he that complies against his will, is of his own opinion still." William Ederington, Fairfield historian.

Time and the river. Time to fish, time to dream, and time to think. Maybe the people in the cities don't fish enough.

An inch of snow, a frosty morning, and a walk from the cabin to the school bus into tomorrow and out of the past in York County.

Over the low, dark shape of Fort Sumter only the sea gulls fly now, except for the flags we may count and see who won the war.

Dusk comes early in November and the street lights of Cheraw flicker on as the stores close. At this same moment, in the freeway traffic of Atlanta, Chicago, or New York, are people who long ago were part of this scene or another very much like it. Perhaps, as they wait for the light to turn and the line of cars to move, there may sometimes be a picture in their mind like this one out of their past.

Early in America's history when the boat came up the Pee Dee River as far as it could and then had to stop for the rocks, Cheraw's founders stepped down the gangplank and constructed buildings with a style and grace that even today make this a town to admire. Lafayette and Sherman walked these streets and there are those yet unborn who will know them well.

It is a place where people still have time to live reflectively and kindly, where neighbor still knows neighbor, where people really believe in the God of their forefathers, and worship in buildings built by the hands of their ancestors.

If there is a heritage and way of life worth saving in today's America, it may well be in places like Cheraw.

No longer king, cotton is still an amazing plant. It will grow not only in the sandy soil of the coastal plains but in the red clay of the upcountry. First there was indigo, then rice, then cotton came dispensing wealth, but also suffering, to both white and black hands and minds.

Opposite: *It was from this courthouse in Newberry where two present-day residents of the town pose that word went out almost a hundred years ago to the day to get your gun and come to Newberry. Not by a single Paul Revere but by a hundred fanning out in all directions in 1876 to rescue the state from the reign of the carpetbaggers. And the people responded. Every man, boy, and even some women, who could ride a horse and carry a rifle, arrived at the Newberry town square at high noon. Rank upon rank of mounted cavalry in perfect order. This apparition, this ghost of Hampton's Legion greeted the motley band of Governor Chamberlain and his disreputable entourage coming to begin the campaign of 1876. The governor made his speech from this balcony but fear had turned to desperation and for the first time in over a decade of military occupation the people of South Carolina were ready to resist their governor from Massachusetts and offer an opposition candidate. Freedom from oppressive taxation, government corruption, injustice—their hope rode with Wade Hampton.*

Opposite: *The spire of St. Philip's Episcopal Church in Charleston.*

The bridges of Charleston with the Cooper River in the distance and the Ashley River in the foreground mark the boundaries north and south. And between the two rivers is the past—Old Charleston, the diadem of historic cities—where no high-rises yet deface the skyline.

ON THIS FIELD AMERICAN TROOPS
UNDER
BRIGADIER GENERAL DANIEL MORGAN
WON A SIGNAL VICTORY OVER A
BRITISH FORCE COMMANDED BY
LIEUTENANT COLONEL BANASTRE TARLETON
JANUARY 17, 1781.

Driving west on South Carolina 11 from Gaffney, a granite marker looms at a small intersection upon a single acre. It is all that has been preserved of the battlefield. Contemporary accounts speak of the bitter cold the night before, the long wait in the darkness for the British. All the wintertime soldiers were not at Valley Forge.

24372